Gooseberry Patch®

W9-CQF-351

HOMEMADE
Harvest

Gooseberry Patch
600 London Road
P.O. Box 190
Delaware, OH 43015

www.gooseberrypatch.com

1·800·854·6673

Copyright 2010, Gooseberry Patch 978-1-936283-01-9
First Printing, March, 2010

Do you have a tried & true recipe...

tip, craft or memory that you'd like to see featured in a **Gooseberry
Patch** cookbook? Visit our website at **www.gooseberrypatch.com**,
register and follow the easy steps to submit your favorite family recipe.
Or send them to us at:

Gooseberry Patch
Attn: Cookbook Dept.
P.O. Box 190
Delaware, OH 43015

Don't forget to include the number of servings your recipe makes,
plus your name, address, phone number and email address.
If we select your recipe, your name will appear right along
with it...and you'll receive a **FREE** copy of the cookbook!

CONTENTS

Dedication

Dedicated to our friends
who love to celebrate the
homemade traditions of fall.

Appreciation

Sending a heartfelt "Thanks"
for all the recipes to savor
and sweet memories to share.

Fall Homecoming

Cyn DeStefano
Mercer, PA

Brisk fall air, colorful russet and golden leaves and football games can only mean one thing...homecoming! In our small town, homecoming is a big celebration. We kick off the big night with a parade that's small in length but huge in heart. The only 2 bands are our own Big Red band and the opposing high school team's band. All of the fall sports teams join in to showcase the year's talent and to kick off what we hope will be a winning season for each of them. The alumni return and march right alongside the band wearing special t-shirts to show they still have Big Red Pride! The finale of the parade is the float carrying the homecoming court. While we may not be a big town, we are big on spirit and heart, and that is always worth coming home to!

Annual Fall Walk

Pamela Chorney
Providence Forge, VA

My husband and I can't wait for fall to arrive each year. We choose a day that has a chill in the air and go walking around Colonial Williamsburg. The leaves have changed from green to beautiful red, gold and orange, and the fallen ones crunch as we walk on them. If it is really chilly, a fire is burning and hot cider is served with ginger cookies...for us, it's a little slice of heaven.

Candy Corn Necklaces

Meg Pyron
Branson, MO

In 1962, our mother made the three of us kids Native American costumes to wear in the town's big Halloween parade. They were very fancy with lots of beading, fringe and patches sewn on for decoration. To complement our costumes, Mom and a friend decided to string candy corn necklaces for each of us to wear. We found that candy corn doesn't string very well...it has a tendency to snap in two just about the time the needle breaks through to the other side. After going through an entire bag of candy and only getting about ten kernels on a necklace, someone finally had the brilliant idea to use a power drill with a small bit to make a hole in the middle of the candy...it worked! What a great memory for us!

A Trick, Not a Treat

Irene O'Donnell
Moline, IL

When I was about twelve years old, a friend and I went trick-or-treating together. We had heard that a certain house, which was on an estate, was handing out large candy bars for Halloween. Filled with excitement, we went to the house wondering what wonderful treat we would get. Instead, after ringing the doorbell, we got a bucket of water thrown on us from an upstairs window! Needless to say, we never went back to that house again.

Gathering Buckeyes

Kathryn Kelley
Mount Vernon, IL

My favorite fall memory has always been collecting buckeyes on the way home from school. I collected hundreds of them, always giving the very best one to my grandfather because he said they brought good luck. Each year, whenever I asked to see the previous year's buckeye, it was always tucked away safely in his pocket.

Pumpkin-Picking Memories

Susan Bick
Ballwin, MO

I grew up in northern Illinois as a child, and autumn was always my favorite time of year. I loved kicking the fallen leaves on the way to school on a crisp fall morning. I remember helping my mom rake the leaves in our yard into a big pile and then jumping in...what fun! My mom always had a warm casserole in the oven or a pot of soup simmering on the stove ready to be relished at dinnertime. My all-time favorite fall memory is when my second grade class went to a pumpkin farm. Pumpkins, scarecrows and other autumn decorations were everywhere! We each got to pick a pumpkin to take home with us to carve. I remember feeling so proud choosing my pumpkin and carrying it back to the school bus. Now, with my own family, we take a trip to the pumpkin patch each fall to carry on the tradition and make memories.

Halloween Photos

Jennifer Levy
Warners, NY

Two years ago we planted a maple tree sapling in our backyard.
Each Halloween, our kids get dressed up in their costumes and head
out to the tree to have their picture taken before trick-or-treating
begins. The pictures are then tucked into a special Halloween photo
album. We're looking forward to seeing how they, and the tree, will
grow over the years. The kids love family traditions like these, and
they'll be able to share the same tradition, and our photos, with
their own kids one day.

Autumn Hayrides

Sherry Nagel
Brook, IN

One of our favorite things to do at our farm is hosting cookouts
and hay rides for family & friends. For many years, we hosted our
church for a cookout, games and evening hayride. Adults could
act like kids again and everyone loved that! Our oldest daughter
directed a preschool reading group, and each fall they came to our
farm for miniature horse rides, leaf gathering, lunch and a hayride.
For many little ones, ours was their first introduction to these great
fall activities. What a wonderful time of year for making memories!

Grandma's Leaf Raking

Dutch Dec
New York, NY

Every Sunday in the fall my grandmother would rake all the leaves
in the garden and put them into trash bags. She would then take
the bags down to the basement and tell us not to go near them.
Then, toward the middle of winter, she would empty the leaves
into a huge compost pile. She explained to us as she did this that
each season rolls into another, just like ingredients in a recipe. She'd
say, "One cup of milk has to come before one tablespoon sugar, but
the milk helps the sugar, just like life." She taught us that the
actions of today would affect the lives of tomorrow.

Time Together

Cindy DeMay
West Springfield, MA

Once my sister arrives at our home for Thanksgiving, she joins
my daughter and me in our truck. We trim berry branches and pines
to fill the window boxes on our homes. We walk through the trees
with a big basket in hand to fill with our treasures. There's always
such a feeling of contentment and joy when we do this. We hope
that my daughter will continue this tradition with her family
someday.

The Leaf Hunt

Beth Schlieper
Lakewood, CO

I grew up in Pennsylvania where the fall leaves are as colorful as the rainbow. When we moved to Colorado sixteen years ago, I always missed the wonderful mix of leaves. Colorado is beautiful, but the fall leaves here are, for the most part, yellow. My mom always sends me an envelope full of leaves to cheer me up. When my three boys were younger, I would give them each a plastic zipping bag and we would go on leaf hunts. We would try to discover as many colorful leaves as possible on our walks. When we were done, we'd come back home and make leaf rubbings. We would always return with as many sticks and rocks as we did leaves! I will never forget their excitement (and mine) when we discovered a red or orange leaf to add to our collection.

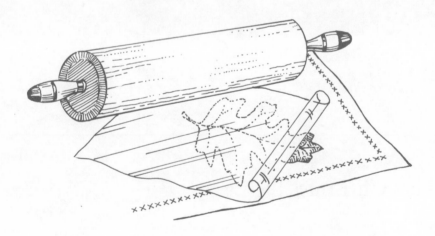

A Thanksgiving Visitor

Shelly Buckley
Powell, TN

While I was growing up, we celebrated Thanksgiving with my dad's
side of the family. I remember we received a phone call from
Grandpa. He had gone to work at the train station on Thanksgiving
morning. That morning he had struck up a conversation with a man
who was stranded and had nowhere to go for Thanksgiving dinner.
So Grandpa called to let my mom know we would need another
plate for Thanksgiving dinner. What a blessing it was to know that
my grandpa loved the joy of food and his family enough to share it
with a man who had no place to go. I am truly blessed that I had
a grandpa who taught me to give with no strings attached.

First Christmas Lights

Diane Stark
Golden, CO

As a child, the part I loved best about spending Thanksgivings at
the home of Mom's aunt and uncle was actually the trip home!
Even though it was always late when we arrived and evening
chores and milking the cows still had to be done, Dad would detour
through town so we could see the Christmas lights on Main Street.

Old-Fashioned Memories

Bonfires

Paula Dabel
Fort Atkinson, WI

My favorite memory of fall is the bonfires. Throughout elementary and high school, it was a tradition for my girlfriends and me to get together for an autumn bonfire. Often we roasted hot dogs and made s'mores, then we'd sing campfire songs and tell stories. Recently, after 40-plus years, we started to get together again to exchange pictures and memories. Our bonfire tradition was certainly a top vote-getter.

Giggling Leaves

Cathy Hergenreder
Pratt, KS

When my two daughters were little and the autumn leaves were falling and blowing down the street, I would say to them, "Girls, look at the leaves, giggling down the street!" Years later, when the girls were older, they would say, "Look Mom, the leaves are giggling again!" Even when they went away to college, we would write to each other and say we saw the leaves giggling and somehow that made us feel as if we were closer to each other. It is a special memory we will always share. So now, whenever you see the leaves twirling and blowing in the wind, tell someone you know, the leaves are giggling!

Grandmother's Tablecloth

Tonya Lewis-Holm
Scottsburg, IN

My grandmother started the tradition of an autographed tablecloth in our family. At the start of the holiday season, she would put out a solid-color cloth for all the guests to sign, date and add a special note. Later, my grandmother would embroider each signature and note. When a tablecloth was filled, she'd put out a new one, but the old ones came out often to remind her of dinners shared with family & friends. Her idea inspired me to do the same at my wedding. Instead of a guest book, I had guests sign an ivory tablecloth and later I embroidered it in my wedding colors.

Cider Pressing

Heather Gingrich
Mercersburg, PA

My favorite fall memory is going with my grandfather to watch apples being pressed to make apple cider. He had a special recipe, combining various types of apples to get the perfect blend. We would take the juicy apples to have them pressed, and from some of that cider, make homemade apple butter in large copper kettles. Nothing tasted better than warm apple butter on my grandma's fresh homemade bread!

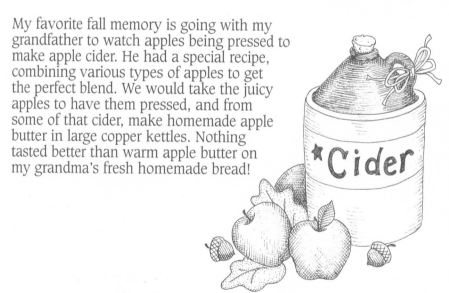

A Family Tradition

Laura Parker
Flagstaff, AZ

Our family makes yummy turkey pot pies after Thanksgiving dinner. Each family will bring a pie plate, and I provide the crusts, peas, carrots and other ingredients to make the pot pies. I have an antique cookie cutter in the shape of a turkey we use to make decorative cuts in the top crust. Each family then gets to take a pot pie home to bake and enjoy for dinner the following week.

Let's Put Up the Tree

Mary Gibis
Vista, CA

Every year after the Thanksgiving dinner, the very minute the last fork was put down, my dad would get a gleam in his eye, look at my mom and say in a fun giggling voice, "Okay, let's put up the Christmas tree!" We would all laugh and know that now the holiday season had arrived at our house!

Autumn Joy

Kristen DeSimone
Peabody, MA

I love autumn! I think about it all year long, and once the 4th of July has passed, I'm ready to start decorating for autumn. It starts in August when I begin putting out my sunflowers and spicy autumn candles. Once September arrives, as far as I am concerned, autumn has begun...out come the pumpkins and fall leaves. I pull out my favorite autumn books and scrapbooks and I begin my annual autumn journal. At the first hint of a cool day, we light the first fire of the season in our fireplace. The first trip to the apple orchard is always a huge treat when my husband and I set aside a Sunday to go to our local orchard. We pick out lots of pumpkins, cornstalks and mums, and we never leave without enjoying a warm cider doughnut. Then comes glorious October...time to add the Halloween decorations to the mix. On November 1st, Halloween is gently put away and my Thanksgiving decor makes its appearance...so many months of fall goodness!

A Mountain Adventure

Linda Taylor
Nebo, KY

One of the fondest memories I have is from about five years ago when my aunt and I were together with ten girlfriends. We went on a trip to the Smoky Mountains in October. We shopped, drove into the mountains to enjoy the scenery and had our pictures taken together. Although my aunt has passed away since then, this wonderful time that we all spent together laughing and joking, is a time I will not soon forget.

Old-Fashioned Memories

Wildlife Hikes

Amanda Johnson
Marysville, OH

As my children grow, it is fun to discover the wildlife around us. We have many state parks near our home and it is always a pleasure to venture out on a crisp fall day and take in all the beautiful surroundings. It's lots of fun to bring a field guide and journal with us to identify the animals we've seen that particular day. The kids love to look back through the journal and talk about the wonder that surrounds us.

A Halloween Parade

Marie Needham
Columbus, OH

I remember riding my pony in a Halloween parade on the main street of my small Ohio hometown. This was about 1940, when I would have been eight years old. My pony Jill was black, and my dad and I wound orange crepe paper around the rings of the martingale, which fit around Jill's neck and chest. It was a nighttime parade and people were carrying Roman candles which provided quite an exciting, mysterious sight. Jill never flinched at the commotion! I shared this memory again with my dad a few years ago, late in his life, and he also remembered it well.

Halloween Fun

Jo Anne Hayon
Sheboygan, WI

When my children were elementary-school age, I would decorate our front porch with carved pumpkins and cobwebs. I would wait until the day of Halloween to put up the cobwebs and get out my cassette tape of spooky sounds. The porch would then be ready for trick-or-treaters and my children would be happy to see the house completely decorated when they arrived home from school that day. I didn't know how much this affected my children until my daughter, who is now 27 years old, mentioned it as one of her favorite memories.

Halloween Window Painting

Maryann Tobin
Duryea, PA

Each year, a few weeks before Halloween, the kids in our town have a Halloween painting contest on various store windows throughout the community. We would first draw a wax outline of our Halloween scene and then fill it in with washable paints. Even though it was often freezing outside, we'd wear warm gloves and create some amazing works of art. Having a cup of hot chocolate and dreaming of winning First Prize helped us through the coldest nights! Once completed, the store windows looked awesome. And as we strolled down Main Street, we enjoyed not only the amazing artwork, but the aroma of warm cider.

Family Movie Night

Carol Hickman
Kingsport, TN

In our family, Halloween night is a family movie night! Each Halloween we enjoy a dinner of Taco Chili and Mexican Cornbread, then we turn off all the lights except for a candle-lit pumpkin. We snuggle up together to watch some of our favorite movies, such as *The Legend of Sleepy Hollow*, *The Ghost and Mr. Chicken* and finally *The Burbs* while snacking on homemade white chocolate snack mix. Even though my children are now 19 and 21 years old, they still insist on continuing our Halloween tradition each and every year.

Harvesting Sweet Corn

Karen Boehme
Greensburg, PA

Growing up in rural Pennsylvania was so much fun. I had my two sisters and two doors down was my aunt who had ten children. At corn harvesting time, we went from our house to theirs to help can corn. My favorite time was at our house where we helped pick, husk and clean the ears. We cut the corn from the cobs and packed it into jars and helped can it. When we were finished, my dad, who held back all the little ears he called "nubbins," would cook them all and reward our work with what seemed like a million ears of corn. We ate until we were full, with salt and butter running down our chins as we ate! We felt that we were so blessed, not only to be helping with something so important, but to be rewarded with the top prize of fresh home-grown sweet corn. To this day, fifty-some years later, when we get together, we talk of those days and how they were one of the best times growing up. Blessings can be such simple things in our lives.

The Syrup Mill

Donna Gay
Summit, MS

When the leaves begin to fall and the mornings get crisp and cool, my thoughts go back to my childhood. Every year in October, my papa would start up the syrup mill. Stalks of sugar cane were harvested and brought to the mill to be crushed, using the juice for making syrup. Through a process of cooking and moving the mixture from one vat down the line to another, the work went on for several weeks. When my three sisters, three cousins and I would get off the school bus, Momma would have a pan of homemade biscuits ready…we could hardly wait to get down that dirt road to the mill where Papa would let us get syrup straight from the vat! Papa has been gone for awhile now, but my memories of him and the syrup mill will always be on my mind this time of year.

Fall Memories

Charlotte Thweatt
Flagstaff, AZ

Our family celebrates the coming of fall on the first day of September. We unwrap bouquets of carefully stored Indian corn, much of it home-grown, and place them on the front door of our home with bows of raffia…a tradition that was begun by my mother over 50 years ago. When fall arrives, we revel in the first scent of wood smoke and anticipate the aroma of my mother's cornbread dressing…the signature of Thanksgiving Day.

Make-Ahead Pumpkin Pie French Toast

Jennifer Yandle
Indian Trail, NC

I combined several different French toast recipes to suit my family's tastes. They love anything with pumpkin, so the pumpkin pie spice was a must. It's a great Sunday morning breakfast...it can bake while you get ready for church. It's also super-easy for husbands to whip up so Mom can sleep in just a bit on Saturday morning!

1 loaf French, Italian, challah
   or Hawaiian bread, cut into
   1-inch slices
3 eggs, beaten
1/2 c. egg substitute
1 c. half-and-half

1-1/2 c. milk
1/4 t. salt
1 t. vanilla extract
1 T. pumpkin pie spice
1/2 c. brown sugar, packed
1 to 2 T. butter, sliced

Arrange bread slices in the bottom of a greased 13"x9" baking pan. Whisk together eggs, egg substitute, half-and-half, milk, salt, vanilla and spice. Stir in brown sugar; pour mixture over bread slices. Refrigerate, covered, overnight. Dot top with butter and bake, uncovered, at 350 degrees for 40 to 45 minutes. Serves 8.

Sprinkle a little pumpkin or apple pie spice over
dollops of whipped cream...yummy on servings
of pancakes, French toast or waffles.

Overnight Coffee Cake

Dee Ann Ice
Delaware, OH

This is a wonderful breakfast to share with family & friends. Prepared the night before, you just pop it in the oven the next morning and settle in to visit while breakfast bakes.

2 c. plus 2 T. all-purpose flour, divided
1 t. baking powder
1 t. baking soda
1/2 t. salt
3/4 c. sugar
1 c. brown sugar, packed and divided

2 t. cinnamon, divided
3/4 c. butter, melted and slightly cooled
1 c. milk
2 eggs, beaten
1/2 c. chopped pecans

Lightly coat a 13"x9" baking pan with non-stick vegetable spray. Add 2 tablespoons flour to pan; shake to spread flour evenly around insides of pan. Stir together remaining flour, baking powder, baking soda, salt, sugar, 1/2 cup brown sugar and one teaspoon cinnamon. Stir in butter, milk and eggs; beat until well combined. Pour into baking pan; cover and refrigerate at least 8 hours, or overnight. When ready to bake, toss together remaining brown sugar and cinnamon with pecans; sprinkle over chilled batter. Bake at 350 degrees for 30 to 35 minutes, or until a wooden toothpick inserted in the center comes out clean. Serves 12 to 15.

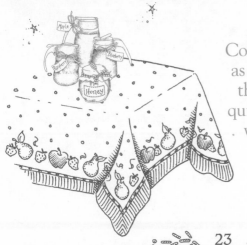

Colorful oilcloth is so pretty as a table covering and has the added bonus of being quick & easy to clean. Ideal when breakfast calls for sticky syrup or honey!

Rise & Shine Frittata

Dale Duncan
Waterloo, IA

*When it's time to harvest on our farm, we start the day early with a
big breakfast...this frittata is always on the menu. After breakfast,
we head out to the fields, kids in tow, and climb into the combine for
a morning of harvesting corn, soybeans or winter wheat.*

6 eggs, beaten
1/3 c. milk
1 T. spicy brown mustard
1/2 t. salt
1/8 t. pepper
1 T. oil

2 c. frozen shredded
   hashbrowns, thawed
1 c. cooked turkey, chopped
1/2 c. green onions, sliced
1/2 c. shredded Cheddar cheese

Whisk together eggs, milk, mustard, salt and pepper; set aside.
Heat oil in a skillet over medium heat; stir in potatoes and cook until
golden. Add turkey and onions; stir to combine. Reduce heat to low
and cook, covered, 3 minutes. Uncover, stir egg mixture and pour
over potatoes. Cover and cook 10 minutes, or until eggs are set. Lift
edges of eggs so uncooked egg flows underneath to cook. Sprinkle
with cheese; cover and continue cooking until cheese melts and
eggs are set. Cut into wedges to serve. Makes 4 servings.

Farmers' markets are open through the fall season,
so don't miss out on all the goodies for a harvest breakfast.
You'll find fresh eggs, syrup, potatoes for hashbrowns
or potato cakes and loads of other veggies for a
tasty omelet or quiche.

24

Ashton Family Quiche

Lisa Ashton
Aston, PA

My kids love quiche and French fries, so I created this recipe for them!

1 c. cooked ham, chopped
9-inch pie crust
1-1/2 c. shredded sharp
    Cheddar cheese
2 T. all-purpose flour
1 c. half-and-half

4 eggs, beaten
salt and pepper to taste
2 c. frozen seasoned French
    fries, thawed and cut into
    bite-size pieces

Arrange ham in the bottom of pie crust; sprinkle with cheese then flour. Whisk together half-and-half, eggs, salt and pepper; fold in French fries. Pour mixture evenly over cheese layer. Bake at 350 degrees for 30 to 40 minutes, until center is set. Serves 8.

Enjoy breakfast outdoors in the crisp fall air! Toss some hay bales around a roomy farmhouse table and invite friends to join you. Tie up place settings with cheery bandannas...they'll double as super-size napkins, then settle in for a great start to the day.

Cranberry-Orange Scones

Joyce LaMure
Sequim, WA

I received this recipe from a friend a few years ago. They're
not only yummy, but quick & easy to make.

2 c. biscuit baking mix
1/2 c. sugar
1/2 c. butter, softened
1 egg, beaten
1/2 c. dried cranberries
1/2 c. chopped pecans

1 T. orange zest
2-1/2 to 3 T. buttermilk or
   light cream
Garnish: beaten egg white,
   raw or sanding sugar

Combine baking mix, sugar and butter until crumbly. Make a well
in the center and add one egg; stir to blend. Stir in cranberries,
pecans and zest. Add buttermilk or cream as needed for dough to
form a soft ball. Place dough on lightly floured surface and knead
3 or 4 times. Flatten dough and shape into an 8-inch circle. Using
a serrated knife, cut dough in triangles. Brush with egg white and
garnish with sugar. Arrange on a lightly oiled baking sheet and bake
at 400 degrees for 10 to 15 minutes, or until golden. Serves 8 to 10.

Toss a few logs in the fireplace…a crackling fire will warm
everyone right up on a brisk fall morning.

Jill's Banana Butter

Jill Ball
Highland, UT

This is a great breakfast butter...I spread it on toast, English muffins and bagels. I even like to give a crock of this butter along with fresh bagels as a yummy birthday breakfast.

4 ripe bananas, sliced	1-1/2 c. sugar
3 T. lemon juice	1 t. pumpkin pie spice

Place bananas and lemon juice in a food processor; pulse until smooth. Transfer mixture to a saucepan and stir in remaining ingredients. Bring to a boil over medium-high heat. Reduce heat and simmer 15 minutes; stir often. Spoon into an airtight container; cover and keep refrigerated. Makes 3 cups.

Peanut Butter-Honey Spread

Mary Schrock
Seaton, IL

This tastes absolutely great on toast!

1/4 c. creamy peanut butter	1/3 c. honey
1/4 c. margarine, softened	1/4 t. cinnamon
1/2 c. powdered sugar	

Beat all ingredients together until fluffy. Spoon into an airtight container; cover and keep refrigerated. Makes 1-1/2 cups.

A pint-size Mason jar filled with homemade fruit butter or sweet spread makes a delightful (and yummy) gift to share with co-workers and neighbors. Use a bit of jute or raffia to tie on a pretty spreader.

Mother's Maple Spice Granola

Hannah Hopkins
Plainfield, VT

I come from a family of six kids. We all enjoyed our mother's delicious home cooking and this was one of my favorite breakfasts.

3/4 c. maple syrup
3/4 c. butter, melted
1 t. vanilla extract
1 t. cinnamon
1 t. nutmeg

1-1/2 c. sweetened flaked
  coconut
1/3 c. sesame seed
1 c. raisins
1/2 c. chopped walnuts

Mix maple syrup and butter thoroughly in a large bowl; add vanilla and spices. Toss remaining ingredients together; stir into syrup mixture. Spoon into a greased 13"x9" baking pan. Bake at 350 degrees for 45 minutes, stirring every 15 minutes. Cool for 10 minutes before serving. Serves 6.

You'll want to be up bright & early for autumn barn sales and auctions. Take along easy-to-snack-on goodies so you don't miss a thing. Fresh or dried fruit, granola, peanut butter crackers and juice boxes are the perfect early morning grab & go snacks.

Best-Ever Breakfast Bars

Mary Ann Lewis
Olive Branch, MS

My husband won't eat cereal for breakfast, but loves these bars! This is a quick & easy, versatile recipe...if your family doesn't like nuts, use chocolate chips or coconut instead. I like using a combination of walnuts and almonds, but you can use peanuts, cashews or pecans. For the dried fruit, try raisins, apples, cherries, pineapple, mango or a combination of several.

1 c. granola
1 c. quick-cooking oats, uncooked
1/2 c. all-purpose flour
1/8 t. cinnamon
1/4 c. brown sugar, packed
1 c. nuts, coarsely chopped
1/2 c. dried fruit, chopped into small pieces
2 T. ground whole flaxseed meal
1/3 c. canola oil
1/3 c. honey
1/2 t. vanilla extract
1 egg, beaten

Combine granola, oats, flour, cinnamon, brown sugar, nuts, fruit and flaxseed meal in a large bowl. Whisk together oil, honey and vanilla; stir into granola mixture. Add beaten egg; stir to blend. Press mixture into a parchment paper-lined 8"x8" baking pan. Bake at 325 degrees for 30 to 35 minutes, or until lightly golden around the edges. Remove from oven and set aside 30 minutes to one hour to cool. Slice into bars. Serves 8 to 12.

Good Neighbor Day is always the fourth Sunday in September. The fall weather is ideal, so make it a day to visit and chat with neighbors, then enjoy a neighborhood potluck outdoors.

Autumn Morning Casserole

Laura Witham
Anchorage, AK

I love the fall...it's my favorite time of year! It's the best when we're cuddled on the couch looking at the leaves and watching the birds preparing for the coming winter.

1/2 lb. maple-flavored ground
   pork breakfast sausage
1 onion, grated
2 cloves garlic, grated
salt and pepper to taste
1/4 c. apple juice
6 slices bread, cubed

3 eggs, beaten
1 c. milk
1 T. mustard
1 t. hot pepper sauce
1-1/2 c. shredded Cheddar
   cheese

Brown sausage in a skillet over medium-high heat; drain and stir in onion, garlic, salt and pepper. Pour apple juice into skillet; stir and cook over medium heat until juice evaporates. Arrange bread cubes in a lightly greased 9"x9" baking pan. Whisk together eggs, milk, mustard and hot sauce. Layer sausage mixture evenly over bread; top bread and sausage with egg mixture. Sprinkle with cheese. Bake, uncovered, at 350 degrees for 35 to 40 minutes, or until eggs are set. Makes 4 to 6 servings.

Be sure to stop at roadside stands along the country roads. You'll find fun pumpkin names, such as Cinderella, Big Max and Baby Boo, alongside gooseneck and apple gourds.

Sausage & Cherry Tart with Walnuts

Sharon Demers
Dolores, CO

This tart is perfect for brunches and teas. The combination of flavors is wonderful!

1 c. all-purpose flour
2/3 c. walnuts, ground
1 T. sugar
1/4 t. salt
1/2 t. dry mustard
1/8 t. cayenne pepper
6 T. chilled butter, cubed
1 to 2 T. milk
1/2 lb. ground pork breakfast
  sausage

1 onion, finely diced
1/2 to 1 c. dried tart cherries
  or cranberries
1/2 c. chopped walnuts
1/4 t. dried thyme
2 eggs, beaten
1 c. whipping cream
3-oz. pkg. crumbled
  Gorgonzola cheese

Combine flour, ground walnuts, sugar, salt, mustard, cayenne pepper and butter in a food processor. Pulse just until mixture resembles bread crumbs. Add one tablespoon milk; pulse until dough comes together. If dough is too crumbly, add more milk until it holds together. Shape dough into a ball and press evenly into a lightly greased 9" round tart pan. Freeze for 30 minutes. Bake crust at 350 degrees for 15 to 20 minutes, or until golden. Remove from oven and set aside. Brown sausage and onion in a skillet over medium heat; drain well. Stir in cherries or cranberries, walnuts and thyme. Set aside. Combine eggs and cream; whisk until smooth. Spoon sausage mixture into baked crust; sprinkle with cheese. Pour egg mixture over all. Bake at 350 degrees for 15 to 20 minutes, or until golden and center tests done. Cool 15 minutes before serving. Makes 8 servings.

Stemless Cinderella pumpkins work perfectly as pedestals for trays filled with fruit slices, cheese or veggies!

Patti's Breakfast Pizza

Patti Walker
Mocksville, NC

Being on the PTO at my children's school meant I was able to serve the staff members breakfast many mornings to thank them for their hard work. This breakfast pizza became a favorite of my family and staff members. Give it a try and I promise you'll love it!

8-oz. tube refrigerated crescent rolls
2 c. shredded Colby-Jack cheese
1/2 c. mayonnaise
1 tomato, peeled and chopped

6 slices bacon, crisply cooked and crumbled
1/2 green pepper, finely chopped
1/4 c. fresh chives, snipped

Press crescent roll dough into a lightly greased 15" pizza pan, making sure to seal all edges. Mix cheese with mayonnaise; spread over dough. Sprinkle bacon over cheese; top with remaining ingredients. Bake at 350 degrees for 30 minutes. Allow to cool slightly; cut into slices. Serves 6 to 8.

Get together with girlfriends and spend a night or two making a quick-stitch autumn apron. A trip to the fabric store will send you home with oodles of fabrics in russet red, harvest gold and even some just-for-fun Halloween prints!

Spicy Ranch Egg Burritos

Darcy Geiger
Columbia City, IN

I created this super-quick recipe...my family loves them!

2 T. oil
1 onion, diced
1 to 1-1/2 doz. eggs, beaten
1/2 c. milk

4 slices Pepper Jack cheese
6 to 8 8-inch flour tortillas
Garnish: spicy ranch salad
 dressing

Heat oil in a skillet over medium-high heat. Stir in onion and cook 3 to 5 minutes. Combine eggs with milk; pour over onion. Cook and stir until eggs are cooked through; layer on cheese and stir. Spoon mixture evenly into the center of each tortilla; roll and top with desired amount of dressing. Serves 6 to 8.

Serve breakfast burritos in flavorful wraps for a tasty change. There are so many flavors that pair up perfectly with eggs...try Pepper-Jack cheese, spinach, tomato-basil and salsa.

Pumpkin Sweet Rolls

Kathryn Hosteler
West Farmington, OH

These are wonderful for breakfast!

1 env. active dry yeast
1-1/4 c. warm milk
1 c. canned pumpkin
1/2 c. sugar
1-1/4 c. butter, divided
1 t. salt
7-1/4 c. all-purpose flour,
   divided

1 c. brown sugar, packed
1-1/2 t. cinnamon
1 c. powdered sugar
1 to 2 T. milk
1/2 t. vanilla extract

In a large bowl, dissolve yeast in milk warmed to 110 to 115 degrees.
Add pumpkin, sugar, 1/2 cup melted butter, salt and 4-3/4 cups
flour. Beat until smooth. Stir in enough of remaining flour to form
a soft dough (up to one cup); dough will be sticky. On a floured
surface, knead dough until smooth and elastic, about 6 to 8
minutes. Place in a greased bowl; turn to grease the top of dough.
Cover and let rise in a warm place until double in size, about one
hour. Punch dough down. Roll into a 24-inch by 10-inch rectangle.
For streusel, combine 1-1/2 cups flour, brown sugar, cinnamon and
3/4 cup cold butter; set aside one cup. Sprinkle remaining streusel
over dough and press down lightly. Roll up jelly-roll style, starting
with the long side. Cut into 24 slices. Place cut-side down in
2 greased 13"x9" baking pans. Sprinkle with reserved streusel.
Cover and let rise until double, about 30 minutes. Bake at
375 degrees for 20 to 25 minutes, or until golden. Combine
powdered sugar, milk and vanilla; drizzle over rolls. Serve warm.
Makes 2 dozen rolls.

Give sweet recipes, mugs of warm cider and
chocolatey cocoa an added sprinkle of pumpkin
or apple pie spice for a yummy, fall flavor.

Supreme Caramel Apple Rolls

Tracey Graham
Churubusco, IN

This recipe is one of my family's most-requested recipes. One time after serving them, one of my seven brothers told me, "These rolls are so bad, I need to take the rest home with me to eat!"

21-oz. can apple pie filling
1/2 c. caramel ice cream
  topping
Optional: 1/2 c. chopped pecans
8-oz. pkg. cream cheese,
  softened

1/3 c. powdered sugar
2 8-oz. tubes refrigerated
  crescent rolls
1/2 c. sugar
1/2 c. brown sugar, packed
1/2 c. butter, melted

Combine pie filling and ice cream topping; pour into a greased 13"x9" baking pan. Sprinkle pecans, if using, over mixture. Combine cream cheese and powdered sugar; set aside. Separate crescent roll dough into 2 rectangles; press perforations to seal. Spread half the cream cheese mixture over each rectangle. Starting with the long side of each rectangle, roll up and seal edges. With a serrated knife, cut each roll into 12 slices. Stir together sugar and brown sugar; dip slices in butter and coat with sugar mixture. Arrange slices in baking pan. Bake at 400 degrees for 25 to 30 minutes, until center rolls are golden. Immediately invert onto a serving plate. Serve warm. Makes 2 dozen rolls.

Plan a harvest scavenger hunt for the whole family. Send them out with a list of fall finds...a golden oak leaf, a russet-red maple leaf, a pumpkin, a scarecrow, a red apple and a hay bale, just to name a few. It's not only lots of fun, it's a great way to get outside and enjoy the fabulous fall weather!

Savory Breakfast Bake

Beth Bundy
Long Prairie, MN

So easy because you prepare it the night before. What could be better than waking up and breakfast is ready to bake?

16-oz. pkg. frozen shredded
   hashbrowns
1 lb. ground pork sausage,
   browned and drained
6 eggs, beaten
1-1/2 c. milk

3/4 t. dry mustard
1/2 t. salt
1/8 t. pepper
1-1/2 c. shredded Cheddar
   cheese

Place hashbrowns into a greased 13"x9" baking pan and layer with sausage. Stir together remaining ingredients except cheese and pour over sausage. Top casserole with cheese; refrigerate overnight. Bake, uncovered, at 350 degrees for 45 minutes. Cool 10 minutes before slicing. Serves 15.

Fall is definitely sweater weather, so keep a cozy sweater
on a hook near the back door and enjoy an
early-morning walk after breakfast.

Harvest Breakfast Casserole

Peggy Moore
Northwood, OH

A favorite dish that's often requested for family gatherings. You don't even need to thaw the broccoli...it keeps the casserole nice and moist.

1 lb. ground turkey breakfast
   sausage
1 t. red pepper flakes
1 doz. eggs, beaten
3-oz. pkg. turkey bacon bits

16-oz. pkg. frozen cut or
   chopped broccoli
2 c. shredded Pepper Jack
   cheese

Brown sausage in a large skillet; sprinkle in pepper flakes. Drain sausage. Combine sausage and remaining ingredients in an extra-large bowl; stir well. Add mixture to a lightly greased 13"x9" baking pan. Bake, uncovered, at 350 degrees for 50 to 60 minutes, until eggs are set. Serves 12.

Pack the cooler and pile everyone in the car for an afternoon of leaf peeping! Stop at roadside stands, look for barn sales and just wander the backroads... a day that's sure to make memories.

Pumpkin Biscotti

Wendy Lee Paffenroth
Pine Island, NY

Slices of biscotti are so nice to give to a co-worker along with a teabag...a welcome morning treat. Try a gingerbread muffin or quick bread mix too...scrumptious!

4 eggs, beaten
1 c. butter, melted and slightly
  cooled
1 t. vanilla extract
2 15.4-oz. pkgs. pumpkin
  muffin or quick bread mix

8-oz. pkg. white or milk
  chocolate chips, divided
1 to 3 T. all-purpose flour

In a large bowl, combine eggs, butter and vanilla; stir until well blended. Blend in dry muffin or quick bread mix and 1/2 cup chocolate chips; stir again. Mixture will be sticky. Add enough flour to form a smooth dough; knead on a lightly floured surface for several minutes. Divide dough in half; shape each half into an oval loaf and flatten slightly. Place on a lightly greased baking sheet and bake at 350 degrees for 30 to 40 minutes, or until golden. Remove from oven and set aside to cool 15 to 20 minutes. Using a serrated knife, cut loaves into one-inch thick slices; arrange on baking sheet. Return to oven and continue to bake 15 minutes longer. Remove from oven and set aside to cool. Melt remaining chocolate chips and drizzle over slices; cool. Serves 6 to 8.

Summer's loss seems little, dear, on days like these.
~Ernest Dowson

Mocha Coffee Smoothie

Kathleen Sturm
Corona, CA

These delicious smoothies will give those expensive coffeehouse treats a run for their money.

1 c. milk
7 to 8 ice cubes
2 T. sugar
1 T. instant coffee granules

2 T. chocolate syrup
Garnish: whipped cream,
　grated chocolate

Combine all ingredients except garnish in a blender. Blend until smooth and creamy; pour into 2 tall glasses. Top with whipped cream and grated chocolate. Makes 2 servings.

Nutty Banana Shake

Marsha Overholser
Ash Grove, MO

A tasty way to use ripe bananas.

2 to 3 bananas, peeled and
　frozen
1 c. milk

2 T. creamy or crunchy peanut
　butter
1 T. honey

Slice frozen bananas and place in a blender with remaining ingredients. Blend until smooth and thick. Makes one serving.

Serve up smoothies and shakes in hollowed-out mini pumpkins… just for silly fun!

Pecan French Toast Casserole

Marilyn Morel
Keene, NH

This is a wonderfully tasty casserole for special mornings or if you have overnight company. It's easy to make and melts in your mouth. My family loves it and the entire pan disappears quickly. When I serve this it brings huge smiles from my two young sons! Works best when bread is one day old. If you must use fresh bread, then slice the bread and place the slices on a large plate to dry for at least a couple of hours.

1 loaf French or Italian bread,
   cut into 1-inch slices
1-1/2 c. milk
1-1/2 c. half-and-half

1 t. vanilla extract
1/8 t. nutmeg
1 t. cinnamon

Arrange bread slices in a lightly greased 13"x9" baking pan. Beat together remaining ingredients; pour over bread slices. Cover and refrigerate overnight. In the morning, uncover and spread with Pecan Topping. Bake, uncovered, at 350 degrees for 45 to 55 minutes. Let stand 5 minutes before serving. Makes 6 to 8 servings.

Pecan Topping:

1/2 c. butter, softened
2 T. maple syrup

1 c. dark brown sugar, packed
1 c. chopped pecans

Combine butter and syrup; blend well. Blend brown sugar and chopped pecans; fold in butter mixture.

Apple-Raisin Muffins

Flo Burtnett
Gage, OK

The chopped apple in these muffins keeps them very moist.
They also have a wonderfully spicy flavor that we love.

1 egg
3/4 c. milk
1 c. raisins
1 apple, cored, peeled and
   shredded
1/2 c. oil
1 c. all-purpose flour
1 c. quick-cooking oats,
   uncooked

1/3 c. sugar
1 T. baking powder
1 t. salt
1 t. nutmeg
2 t. cinnamon
Garnish: butter

Whisk egg in a bowl; stir in remaining ingredients just until moistened. Mixture will be lumpy. Fill 12 greased or paper-lined muffin cups 3/4 full. Bake at 400 degrees for 15 to 20 minutes. Serve warm, topped with butter. Makes one dozen.

A friend with the sniffles will love it when you deliver a basket of home-baked muffins to her door. Tuck a cozy neck warmer in the basket too. So simple...just fill a colorful new knee sock with uncooked rice, then tie a ribbon on the open end to keep it securely closed. She can heat it up in the microwave for one minute and place it around her neck...so comforting.

Easy Biscuits & Gravy

Mary Jane Calas
Chicago, IL

I love serving my family biscuits and gravy on a crisp fall morning.

1/2 to 1 lb. sage-flavored
   ground pork breakfast
   sausage
2 T. butter
1/4 c. all-purpose flour

4 c. milk, or 3 c. milk and
   1 c. half-and-half
salt and pepper to taste
8 buttermilk biscuits, baked
   and split

Brown sausage in a large skillet over medium-high heat; drain.
Remove sausage from skillet; set aside on paper towels to drain.
Add butter to skillet over medium heat; stir to melt. Add flour; stir
continuously until mixture thickens. Reduce heat to medium-low
and slowly add milk. Stir constantly until mixture is thick and
bubbly. Return sausage to skillet; season with salt and pepper as
desired. Serve over biscuits. Makes 4 servings.

Farmhouse Sausage Patties

Debbie Raynes
Johnstown, OH

*Adding my own special ingredients to plain sausage really makes it
taste terrific. It's great crumbled for sausage gravy or shaped into
patties with eggs and hashbrowns for a real country breakfast.*

1 lb. ground pork
1 t. ground cumin
1/2 t. dried thyme
1/2 t. dried sage

1 t. salt
1/2 t. pepper
Optional: 1/8 t. cayenne pepper

Combine all ingredients; mix well. Cover and refrigerate overnight
to allow flavors to blend. Form into 6 patties. Arrange in a lightly
greased skillet and brown both sides over medium heat. Serves 6.

WARM &
INVITING
Soups & Breads

Turkey & Dressing Soup

Cathy Garrett
Balch Springs, TX

In the past, I've used chicken breast in place of turkey...it's really tasty with either. All my family loves this soup, especially served with warm cornbread.

2-1/2 lb. turkey breast
10 c. water
2 carrots, peeled and chopped
3 c. celery, chopped and divided
2 onions, chopped and divided
2 bay leaves

1 t. salt
1/2 t. pepper
1-1/2 t. dried sage
1 t. poultry seasoning
Garnish: 2 eggs, hard-boiled,
    peeled and sliced

Combine turkey, water, carrots, 2 cups celery, one onion and bay leaves in a Dutch oven. Season with salt and pepper. Bring to a boil over medium-high heat; reduce heat and simmer 1-1/2 hours. Remove turkey; set aside. When cool enough to handle, remove meat from bones and chop; discard skin. Strain broth and discard vegetables; return to Dutch oven with chopped turkey. Stir in remaining celery, onion, sage and poultry seasoning; bring to a boil. Reduce heat and simmer, uncovered, 45 minutes. Garnish with egg slices. Serves 10 to 12.

Garden centers are overflowing in the fall with flowers that love the brisk fall weather. Bring home lots of mums and pansies...you're sure to find them in your favorite colors.

Slow-Cooker Autumn Stew

Rachel Boyd
Defiance, OH

One evening I made a campfire bundle out of chicken, potatoes, butternut squash and peppers. It was so good, I thought I would try it in the slow cooker with turkey, sweet potatoes, potatoes and squash... it turned out even better! Served with buttermilk biscuits and honey, it's a yummy meal that will warm you to your toes.

2 butternut squash, peeled
   and diced
4 potatoes, peeled and
   quartered
2 sweet potatoes, peeled and
   quartered
2 c. buttermilk

14-1/2 oz. can beef broth
1/8 t. ground cloves
1/2 t. cinnamon
28-oz. can turkey, drained
1/2 t. dried sage
1 t. dried parsley
1/4 c. cornstarch

Arrange squash and potatoes in a slow cooker; pour in buttermilk and beef broth. Sprinkle vegetables with cloves and cinnamon. Add turkey; sprinkle with sage and parsley. Cover and cook on high setting 5 hours, or until potatoes are tender. Whisk in cornstarch and cook until sauce thickens. Serves 8 to 10.

Slow cookers are ideal for hearty soups and stews.
For quick clean-up, add a disposable slow-cooker liner
before adding ingredients, or give the inside of the cooker
a good coating of non-stick vegetable spray.

Old-Timer Beef Stew

Ben Gothard
Jemison, AL

This dish is just right with a hot grilled cheese sandwich or crisp cornbread. Spoon into a thermos for cool-weather outings such as football games or hayrides. It even freezes well and tastes good reheated. You can even enjoy a slow-cooker version of this soup... simply cook on the low setting for 6 hours, then add the flour to thicken as instructed. Enjoy!

2 lbs. stew beef, cubed
1/2 c. margarine
1 T. garlic salt
1 T. pepper
2 lbs. potatoes, cubed
4 carrots, peeled and sliced
1 to 2 onions, chopped
4 stalks celery, chopped

1 c. frozen green peas
1 c. frozen corn
2 14-1/2 oz. cans diced
   tomatoes
1-1/2 c. catsup
12-1/2 c. water, divided
1/2 c. all-purpose flour

Place beef, margarine, garlic salt, pepper, vegetables, catsup and 12 cups water in a large stockpot; bring to a boil. Reduce heat and simmer, covered, 35 to 45 minutes or until beef is tender. Whisk flour and remaining water in a bowl. When vegetables are tender, carefully remove 2 cups of hot broth and whisk into the flour mixture to thicken; stir until smooth and return to stockpot. Simmer 10 minutes. Makes 12 servings.

Autumn stews are oh-so festive served up in hearty bread bowls or hollowed-out sugar pumpkins. Hollow out a large Cinderella pumpkin as a soup tureen...what fun!

Herb Bread

Cara Lorenz
Olathe, CO

My sister-in-law shared this delicious recipe with me. It is very easy to stir up and makes the kitchen smell so good while it's baking.

1 env. active dry yeast	1 t. garlic salt
1-3/4 c. warm water	1/2 t. dried oregano
4 c. all-purpose flour	1/2 t. dried basil
3 T. sugar	1/2 t. dried parsley
1 t. salt	Garnish: melted butter

Add yeast to warm water, 110 to 115 degrees; stir to dissolve. Blend in remaining ingredients except butter; stir until smooth. Cover with a tea towel; set aside until double in bulk. Punch down and turn dough out on a lightly floured surface. Knead until smooth and bubbles have disappeared. Divide dough in half and shape into 2 loaves. Place in 2 greased 9"x5" loaf pans; cover and let rise again until double. Bake at 350 degrees for 35 to 40 minutes. Remove from pans and brush with butter. While bread is still warm, place in plastic zipping bags to keep moist. Makes 2 loaves.

Bread machines are terrific for baking up loaves of delicious homemade bread. Converting your favorite homemade bread recipe to a bread machine recipe is fairly simple too. If your homemade bread recipe makes 2 loaves of bread, simply halve all the ingredients to use your bread machine. However, don't cut the amount of yeast used, it should remain the same…about 2 teaspoons.

Chocolatey Pumpkin Bread

Jennifer Niemi
Nova Scotia, Canada

Chocolate and pumpkin are a heavenly combination!

4 c. all-purpose flour
4 t. baking powder
1 t. baking soda
1/2 t. salt
1-3/4 c. sugar
2-1/2 t. cinnamon
1-1/2 t. ground cloves
1 t. nutmeg

3 eggs, beaten
28-oz. can pumpkin
2 t. vanilla extract
1 c. oil
1 c. milk
1 c. semi-sweet chocolate chips
1-1/2 c. walnut pieces, toasted

In a large bowl, sift together flour, baking powder, baking soda, salt, sugar, cinnamon, cloves and nutmeg. In a separate bowl, whisk together eggs, pumpkin, vanilla, oil and milk. Pour egg mixture into flour mixture; stir just to moisten. Fold in chocolate chips and walnuts. Divide equally among 3 greased and floured 9"x5" loaf pans. Bake at 350 degrees for 65 minutes, or until a toothpick inserted into the center comes out clean. Makes 3 loaves.

To toast nuts, place them on a lightly oiled baking sheet
and bake at 350 degrees for 7 to 8 minutes. Stir once
during baking time; set aside to cool before adding
to a favorite recipe. Yummy!

Marcia's Pear Bread

Marcia Marcoux
Charlton, MA

You'll love this yummy bread...spread warm slices with real butter or softened cream cheese.

1/2 c. butter
1 c. sugar
2 eggs, beaten
1 t. vanilla extract
1/2 t. salt
1 t. baking powder

1/8 t. nutmeg
2 c. all-purpose flour
1/4 c. buttermilk or plain
  yogurt
1 c. pears, cored, peeled and
  coarsely chopped

Blend butter until smooth; stir in sugar until mixture is creamy. Add eggs and vanilla. Whisk together salt, baking powder, nutmeg and flour; stir into egg mixture alternately with buttermilk. Stir in pears. Pour into a greased 9"x5" loaf pan. Bake at 350 degrees for one hour. Makes one loaf.

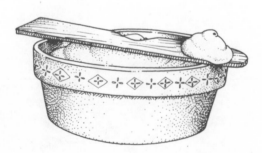

For a fruity cream cheese spread, combine two, 8-ounce packages of softened cream cheese with 1/2 cup apricot or peach preserves; blend until smooth. So delicious on warm slices of quick bread.

Stuffed Green Pepper Soup

*Peggy Cantrell
Okmulgee, OK*

I'm asked for the recipe every time I serve this slow-cooker soup...it's all the flavors of a stuffed green pepper without the work! I serve it with buttery cornbread...a complete meal in itself.

2 lbs. ground beef, browned
   and drained
2 10-3/4 oz. cans tomato soup
28-oz. can petite diced
   tomatoes
4-oz. can mushroom pieces,
   drained

2 c. green pepper, diced
1 c. onion, diced
1/4 c. brown sugar, packed
32-oz. container beef broth
2 c. cooked rice

Combine all ingredients except broth and rice in a slow cooker. Stir in broth as needed until soup is of desired consistency. Cover and cook on low setting 4 to 6 hours, or until pepper and onion are tender. About 15 minutes before serving, stir in rice and heat through. Serves 6 to 8.

Mini BLTs are tasty served alongside bowls of steamy soup.
Toast rounds of bread under the broiler, turn and top
with a slice of cherry tomato, bacon and a dollop
of mayonnaise. Top with a second toasted slice...yum!

Mother's Rolls

Amy Hansen
Louisville, KY

Growing up, we couldn't wait until Mother's rolls were out of the oven and ready to enjoy. Now, with a family of my own, the next generation can hardly wait for them to be cool enough to eat!

1 env. active dry yeast
3/4 c. water
3-1/2 c. biscuit baking mix,
    divided

1 T. sugar
1/4 c. butter, melted

Dissolve yeast in warm water, about 110 to 115 degrees. Add 2-1/2 cups biscuit mix to a large bowl; stir in sugar. Add yeast mixture, stirring vigorously. Sprinkle work surface generously with remaining biscuit mix. Place dough on surface and knead 15 to 20 times. Shape heaping tablespoons of dough into balls; arrange on a lightly greased baking sheet. Cover with a damp cloth; set aside in a warm place to rise, one hour. Brush rolls with melted butter. Bake at 400 degrees for 12 to 15 minutes, or until golden. Remove rolls from oven; brush again with melted butter while hot. Makes 15 rolls.

Decorate your mantel in autumn's best...
cinnamon-scented candles, gourds, bittersweet vines,
Chinese lanterns, colorful leaves and mini pumpkins.

Spicy Beans & Rice Soup

Sarah Gruber
Monroe, MI

Use a leftover ham bone to make this hearty soup...it's a great meal to stretch your grocery budget.

1 T. olive oil
1 onion, diced
2 stalks celery, diced
2 t. garlic, minced
48-oz. jar pinto beans, drained
   and rinsed
14-1/2 oz. can diced tomatoes
   with green chiles

1 meaty ham bone or
   1 to 2 c. cooked ham, diced
1/4 t. pepper
1 t. onion powder
1 t. Cajun seasoning
4 c. water
cooked rice

Add oil to a stockpot over medium-high heat. Stir in onion, celery and garlic; cook until softened. Add remaining ingredients except rice. Simmer 45 minutes. If using ham bone, remove from stockpot and set aside until cool enough to handle. Remove meat, chop and return to soup. Stir to combine; spoon soup over servings of rice. Makes 8 to 10 servings.

Soups are perfect for warming up those little trick-or-treaters before they head out. Add a yummy grilled cheese sandwich and glass of milk and they're all set for an evening of Halloween surprises!

Slow-Cooker Kielbasa Soup

Judy Lange
Imperial, PA

This is a terrific cold-weather soup...warms you right up after a hockey game!

16-oz. pkg. frozen mixed
  vegetables
6-oz. can tomato paste
1 onion, chopped
3 potatoes, diced

1-1/2 to 2 lbs. Kielbasa
  sausage, thinly sliced
4 qts. water
Optional: chopped fresh
  parsley

Combine all ingredients except parsley in a slow cooker. Cover and cook on low setting 10 to 12 hours. Garnish individual servings with parsley, if desired. Serves 8.

The ultimate comfort food...place a scoop of mashed potatoes in the center of a soup bowl, then ladle hearty soup all around the potatoes.

Chicken Tortilla Chowder

Lanita Anderson
Chesapeake, VA

*Our family loves Mexican food and this is a tasty soup recipe that is
similar to one you'd find in a Mexican restaurant.*

4 8-inch flour tortillas
14-1/2 oz. can chicken broth
10-3/4 oz. can cream of
    chicken soup
10-3/4 oz. can cream of potato
    soup
1-1/2 c. milk
2 c. cooked chicken, cubed
11-oz. can sweet corn & diced
    peppers

4-oz. can chopped green chiles
1/4 c. green onions, thinly
    sliced
1-1/2 c. shredded Cheddar,
    Monterey Jack or
    Mexican-blend cheese
Optional: additional cheese,
    sour cream

Lightly spray tortillas with non-stick vegetable spray; arrange on an
ungreased baking sheet. Bake at 375 degrees for 5 to 6 minutes, or
until lightly golden; set aside. Use a pizza cutter to cut tortillas into
1/2-inch strips. Combine broth, soups and milk in a Dutch oven. Stir
in chicken, corn, chiles and onions; mix well. Bring to a boil. Reduce
heat and simmer, uncovered, until heated through. Add cheese; stir
until melted. Ladle soup into serving bowls. Garnish with tortilla
strips, and, if desired, cheese and sour cream. Serves 8 to 10.

Pick up a vintage bike at a tag
sale, wire on a basket and fill it
with autumn's bounty! Line the
bottom of the basket with straw
and top it with mini pumpkins,
birdhouse gourds and ears of
Indian corn. What a colorful
front-porch welcome!

Cornmeal-Cheddar Biscuits

Mary Gage
Wakewood, CA

*If you really like the flavor of Cheddar, try making these biscuits
with extra-sharp Cheddar cheese.*

1-1/2 c. all-purpose flour
1/2 c. yellow cornmeal
2 t. sugar
1 T. baking powder

1/4 to 1/2 t. salt
1/2 c. butter
1/2 c. shredded Cheddar cheese
1 c. milk

Combine flour, cornmeal, sugar, baking powder and salt; cut in
butter until mixture resembles coarse crumbs. Stir in cheese and
milk just until moistened. Drop dough by 1/4 cupfuls onto an
ungreased baking sheet. Bake at 450 degrees for 12 to 15 minutes,
or until lightly golden. Makes one dozen.

Autumn is the best time to think forward to spring flowers.
Plant tulip, crocus, daffodil and hyacinth bulbs when
October comes around and you'll be rewarded in
spring with beautiful flowers!

Country Noodle Soup

JoAnn

*Noodles pair up with fresh veggies for a hearty soup that's
just right for crisp autumn evenings.*

2 T. oil
2 onions, chopped
3 carrots, peeled and chopped
2 stalks celery, sliced into
   1/2-inch pieces
49-oz. container low-sodium
   chicken broth
15-oz. can diced tomatoes

1 T. tomato paste
2-1/2 to 3 c. potatoes, peeled
   and diced
3 c. green beans, halved
1-1/4 t. salt
1 c. wide egg noodles,
   uncooked
1/3 c. fresh parsley, chopped

Add oil to a large saucepan over medium-low heat. Stir in onions,
carrots and celery, stirring occasionally, for 10 minutes. Add
remaining ingredients except noodles and parsley. Bring to a boil,
then reduce heat and simmer, partially covered, 20 minutes.
Stir in noodles; simmer until vegetables and noodles are tender,
about 5 minutes. Stir in parsley. Makes 4 servings.

Now that the weather is not too hot and not too cold, it's
the best time for a family reunion. Send out save-the-date
cards and encourage everyone to bring along their favorite
photos and stories to share. Make plans for a day of fun
and games, along with a lot of sweet memory making.

Fast-Fix Tomato-Basil Soup

*Lynsey Jackson
Maryville, TN*

I like to play in the kitchen, or as my mom fondly calls it, "making potion." This was one of my very successful concoctions and my family requests it regularly!

4 10-3/4 oz. cans tomato soup
2-1/2 c. water
1 c. whipping cream
1 T. chicken bouillon granules

3 T. grated Romano, Asiago &
   Parmesan cheese blend
2 T. dried basil

Add soup to a stockpot over medium heat. Stir in water, whipping cream, bouillon, cheese and basil. Whisk ingredients together and heat through, but do not boil, stirring occasionally. Serves 4 to 6.

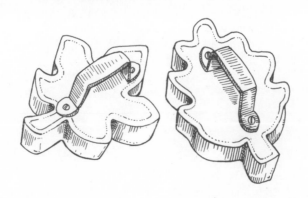

It's so easy to make your own croutons for harvest soups and stews. Toast slices of sourdough bread, then cut out with pumpkin, leaf, bat, ghost or witch's hat cookie cutters.

Maggie's Potato Bread

*Regina Wickline
Pebble Beach, CA*

*When my daughter, Maggie, brought this bread to a soup supper,
it was gone in a flash!*

1 c. milk
3 T. sugar
2 t. salt
3 T. margarine
3/4 c. instant mashed potato
   flakes

2 envs. active dry yeast
1 c. warm water
5-1/2 c. all-purpose flour,
   divided

Scald milk by adding it to a saucepan over medium heat. Bring milk just to boiling; add sugar, salt, margarine and potato flakes. Let cool to lukewarm. In a large bowl, dissolve yeast in warm water, between 110 and 115 degrees. Stir in milk mixture. Add 3 cups flour; beat until smooth. Add enough of remaining flour to form a soft dough. Turn dough out onto a lightly floured surface and knead until smooth, about 8 to 10 minutes. Place in a greased bowl; cover and let rise until double in bulk, about one hour. Punch down and shape into 2 loaves. Place in 2 greased 9"x5" loaf pans; cover and let rise again until double. Bake at 400 degrees for 10 minutes, then reduce temperature to 375 degrees. Continue baking for 30 minutes. Turn bread out onto a wire rack to cool. Makes 2 loaves.

Pick up stencils and acrylic paint at the craft store to easily make your own harvest signs. Stencil on greetings such as "Welcome Fall" or "Happy Harvest." Give finished signs a light sanding and a coat of stain to make them look like barn-sale treasures! If you're going to hang them outside, be sure to brush on several coats of polyurethane to protect them from the weather.

Flo's Cheddar-Apple Bread

Flo Burtnett
Gage, OK

This quick bread is a yummy blend of flavors.

2-1/2 c. all-purpose flour
3/4 c. sugar
2 t. baking powder
1/2 t. salt
1/2 t. cinnamon
2 eggs, beaten
3/4 c. milk

1/3 c. margarine, melted and
  cooled
2 c. shredded Cheddar cheese
1-1/2 c. apples, cored, peeled
  and chopped
3/4 c. chopped nuts

Stir together flour, sugar, baking powder, salt and cinnamon. In
a separate bowl, whisk eggs, milk and margarine. Stir into flour
mixture. Add remaining ingredients; stir to blend. Spoon into a
greased and floured 9"x5" loaf pan. Bake at 350 degrees for 65 to
70 minutes, or until wooden toothpick comes out clean. Set pan
aside to cool 5 minutes before slicing. Makes one loaf.

Bee Butter is oh-so delicious spread over warm split
biscuits and slices of bread. Simply blend together
1/2 cup of softened butter with 2 tablespoons of honey.

Farmstand Cloverleaf Rolls

Brenda Smith
Gooseberry Patch

You'll find all types of squash at the farmstands that dot the country roads this time of year. I like to use Hubbard squash for this recipe, but try any of your favorites too.

1 c. milk
2 T. sugar
1-1/4 t. salt
2 T. shortening

1 env. active dry yeast
3/4 c. winter squash, peeled, cooked and mashed
3-1/2 to 4 c. all-purpose flour

In a saucepan over low heat, combine milk, sugar, salt and shortening; stir until shortening melts. Cool slightly, 120 to 130 degrees; add yeast and stir to dissolve. Blend in squash. Add enough flour to make a soft dough; stir well and place in a greased bowl. Cover with a damp cloth and let rise in a warm place until double in bulk, about 30 minutes. Punch dough down and shape teaspoonfuls of dough into balls about one inch in diameter. Arrange 3 balls in each greased muffin cup. Cover with a damp cloth and let rise in a warm place until nearly double in bulk, about 15 minutes. Bake at 450 degrees for 12 to 15 minutes. Makes 1-1/2 dozen.

A simple harvest touch…bundle silverware into a homespun napkin and tuck in a colorful autumn leaf.

Jennifer's Corn Chowder

Jennifer Niemi
Nova Scotia, Canada

Try topping servings with finely chopped green pepper or chives.

1/4 c. butter	1-1/8 t. pepper
3 c. onion, finely chopped	1/4 t. celery seed
4 c. vegetable broth	1 T. sugar
3 c. potatoes, peeled and cubed	2 12-oz. cans corn
4 to 5 cloves garlic, minced	4 c. milk

Melt butter in a 4-quart saucepan over medium heat. Add onion; cook until translucent. Stir in broth, potatoes, garlic, pepper, celery seed, sugar and corn. Bring to a boil. Reduce heat and simmer, covered, 30 minutes. Stir in milk. Heat to desired temperature, but do not boil. Serves 6.

Fill a simple terra-cotta flowerpot with dried wheat for a quick & easy harvest centerpiece that's also a thoughtful favor for guests. When dinner's over, send friends home with one of their own.

Yummy Banana-Nut Bread

Kristin Turman
Jackson, TN

*I love to make this for breakfast on a cool morning,
or sometimes for an evening snack.*

1/4 c. butter
1/2 c. sugar
1 egg, beaten
1 t. vanilla extract
2 to 3 bananas, mashed

1 c. all-purpose flour
1/2 c. chopped pecans or
  walnuts
Optional: 1/2 c. blueberries

Blend butter and sugar together until creamy; stir in egg and vanilla.
Add mashed bananas and stir well; fold in remaining ingredients.
Pour into a greased 9"x5" loaf pan. Bake at 350 degrees for 30 to
35 minutes, or until golden. Makes one loaf.

Preserve the beauty of autumn leaves…it's easy. Place the
stems in a mixture of one part glycerin to 2 parts water.
After a few days, remove them from the solution and
wipe dry. They're now preserved and ready for
beautiful garlands, bookmarks or wreaths.

Scrumptious Pumpkin Bread

Amy Hunt
Traphill, NC

*My husband and nephews love pumpkin rolls and this is
an easy version of that famous fall treat.*

1 c. canned pumpkin
1 c. plus 2 T. sugar, divided
1/2 c. brown sugar, packed
4 egg whites, divided
1/2 c. fat-free milk
1/4 c. canola oil
2 c. all-purpose flour

2-1/2 t. baking powder
2 t. pumpkin pie spice
1/4 t. salt
1 c. walnut pieces
8-oz. pkg. Neufchâtel cheese,
    softened

Combine pumpkin, one cup sugar, brown sugar, 3 egg whites, milk
and oil in a large bowl. In a separate bowl, sift together flour, baking
powder, pumpkin pie spice and salt; stir into pumpkin mixture just
until moistened. Stir in walnut pieces. Blend together Neufchâtel
cheese, remaining sugar and egg white until smooth. Spoon half the
pumpkin mixture into a greased 9"x5" loaf pan. Spoon Neufchâtel
cheese mixture over pumpkin layer; cover with remaining pumpkin
mixture. Bake at 350 degrees for one hour, or until a wooden
toothpick inserted near the center comes out clean. Cool in pan
for 10 minutes, then remove bread from pan to a wire rack to
finish cooling. Makes one loaf.

Head to the pumpkin
patch, take a wagon ride,
run through a corn maze...
fall is full of wonderful
activities for the young
and young-at-heart!

Creamy Ham & Potato Soup

Hope Davenport
Portland, TX

*This is a quick, easy and delicious soup. My whole family loves it,
so I'm happy to make it often.*

30-oz. pkg. frozen diced
    potatoes
6 c. water
1/3 c. onion, chopped
2 10-3/4 oz. cans cream of
    chicken soup

8-oz. pkg. pasteurized process
    cheese spread, cubed
1 c. sour cream
2 c. cooked ham, cubed
salt and pepper to taste

Combine potatoes, water and onion in a large saucepan. Bring
to a boil over medium-high heat; reduce heat and stir in soup and
cheese. Stir until cheese is melted. Blend in remaining ingredients.
Cook and stir until heated through, but do not boil. Serves 6.

A bonfire is a great harvest tradition. Offer friends bowls
of warming soups, stews and chili along with cornbread
and biscuits. For dessert, roast apples over the fire and
sprinkle with cinnamon-sugar.

Blue-Ribbon Crab & Asparagus Chowder

Patti Bogetti
Magnolia, DE

If you like asparagus, you will love this chowder! The recipe has become a tradition at my friend's annual Barn Bash every fall. Recently, I won the blue ribbon at the state fair in the Chili vs. Chowder Cook-off, yee-haw!

1/2 c. butter
1 sweet onion, chopped
2 carrots, peeled and chopped
3 stalks celery, chopped
1 t. salt
1/2 t. pepper
1/4 c. all-purpose flour
4 c. water
1/2 t. nutmeg
1 t. seafood seasoning

1 T. chicken bouillon granules
3 to 4 redskin potatoes, peeled and cubed
4 c. half-and-half
2 t. fresh parsley, chopped
2-1/2 to 3 c. asparagus, trimmed and chopped
1 lb. crabmeat
Optional: additional half-and-half

Melt butter in a large stockpot over medium heat; add onion, carrots, celery, salt and pepper. Continue to cook until vegetables are softened, about 10 minutes. Stir in flour to coat vegetables. Slowly whisk in water; stir in nutmeg, seasoning, bouillon and potatoes. Bring to a boil; reduce heat and simmer, covered, 10 minutes or until potatoes are tender. Add half-and-half, parsley and asparagus. Simmer 10 minutes longer. Gently fold in crabmeat. Heat through. If chowder is too thick, thin with more half-and-half, if desired. Serves 8 to 10.

Change up a favorite soup recipe. Arrange oven-safe soup bowls on a jelly-roll pan and place thick slices of crusty bread in the bottom of each bowl. Ladle warm soup over bread to fill the bowl. Add a slice of cheese over soup and broil until cheese is bubbly.

Caesar Toast

Gladys Kielar
Perrysburg, OH

This is our family favorite with Caesar salad.

1 egg, beaten
1/4 c. Caesar salad dressing
8-oz. tube refrigerated
  crescent rolls

2 c. herb-flavored stuffing
  mix, crushed
1/3 c. grated Parmesan cheese

Combine egg and salad dressing; mix well. Unroll crescent dough and separate into 8 triangles. Cut each one in half lengthwise, forming 16 triangles. Dip each triangle into salad dressing mixture. Coat both sides of triangle with crushed stuffing. Place one inch apart on an ungreased baking sheet; sprinkle with Parmesan cheese. Bake at 375 degrees for 12 to 15 minutes, until golden. Makes 16.

This harvest season, share a jar of Seed Soup with friends & neighbors. In early fall, catch the seeds from dried flowers and save them in little jam jars. Store the jars in a cool, dry place, shaking them from time to time. When you're ready to give them away, secure lids and tie on a tag that lists the flower names.

Garlic Bread Ring

Patty Fosnight
Childress, TX

This a recipe you can turn to and "wow" dinner guests! They won't believe you used refrigerated biscuits.

1/2 c. butter
2 to 3 cloves garlic, pressed
1 T. Italian seasoning

3 12-oz. tubes refrigerated
country-style biscuits
1/4 c. grated Parmesan cheese

Melt butter in a saucepan over medium heat; stir in garlic and seasoning. Arrange biscuits on their sides in an ungreased Bundt® pan. Pour butter mixture over biscuits. Bake at 350 degrees for 30 to 35 minutes. Invert biscuits onto a plate and top with cheese. Pull apart to serve. Serves 8.

Drill holes that are just big enough to tuck battery-operated candles into the tops of pumpkins. Pile several into a wheel barrow or wagon for a harvest welcome.

Kathie's Beef & Barley Soup

Kathie Poritz
Burlington, WI

I make this soup ahead to have ready for the end of a shopping day. My grown daughters and I put our feet up and rest. When we're ready for dinner, all I have to do is reheat the soup. You can also substitute any favorite vegetable for the turnip if you'd prefer.

1 to 2-lb. beef shank	1/4 t. dried thyme
1/4 c. celery, diced	8 c. water
2 T. fresh parsley, chopped	1/2 c. pearled barley
salt to taste	1 c. turnip, peeled and diced
2 t. Worcestershire sauce	1 c. carrots, peeled and sliced
1 bay leaf	1/2 c. onion, chopped

In a large stockpot over medium-high heat, combine beef, celery, parsley, salt, sauce, bay leaf, thyme and water. Cover and bring to a boil; reduce heat and simmer 2 hours. Remove beef from broth; set aside. When cool enough to handle, cut off meat and dice. Strain broth and return to stockpot; stir in barley and simmer, covered, 30 minutes. Add remaining vegetables and beef; simmer until vegetables are tender, about 30 minutes. Serves 6 to 8.

When you find you have leftover soup, ladle 2-cup portions into freezer bags...seal, label and freeze. Then, when you need a quick-fix dinner, simply let family members choose a bag, transfer soup to a microwave-safe bowl and reheat.

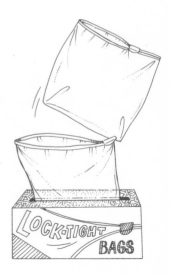

SAVORY
Suppers

Maple-Pineapple Ham

Andrea Heyart
Aubrey, TX

This recipe came about during my first few weeks of marriage. I wanted to create something special for my new husband and decided to combine some of his favorite foods together as a glaze for the ham I had bought. Now every year around our anniversary I make this dish and bring back some of those newlywed memories!

1 c. brown sugar, packed
1 c. maple syrup
3/4 c. pineapple juice
1/4 c. applesauce
1 t. brown mustard

1/2 t. ground cloves
1/2 t. allspice
1/2 t. pumpkin pie spice
6 to 8-lb. cooked bone-in ham

Combine all ingredients except ham; stir to blend. Place ham in an ungreased roasting pan. Brush ham with half of the brown sugar mixture. Bake, uncovered, at 325 degrees for 18 to 24 minutes per pound. Spoon remaining mixture over individual servings. Serves 6 to 8.

Fill a vintage wooden tool caddy with fragrant dried apple and orange slices, star anise and bay leaves, then tuck candles into glass votive holders for a soft glow. What a cozy harvest welcome on a farmhouse table!

Fancy Dressed-Up Potatoes

Cynde Sonnier
Mont Belvieu, TX

Whenever we have a birthday or special occasion, my family always asks for this delicious side dish.

5 lbs. potatoes, peeled
   and quartered
1/2 c. butter, divided
1/2 c. green pepper, chopped
1/2 c. roasted red pepper,
   chopped
1/2 c. onion, chopped

2 to 3 cloves garlic, minced
1/4 c. fresh parsley, chopped
3/4 c. whipping cream
1/4 lb. pasteurized processed
   cheese, cubed
salt and pepper to taste

Add potatoes to a large saucepan. Cover with water and boil over medium-high heat until potatoes are tender; drain. Set aside and keep warm. Add 1/4 cup butter to a saucepan over medium heat; sauté peppers and onion until tender. Add garlic and parsley. Add potatoes to saucepan with 1/4 cup butter and remaining ingredients. Mash with a fork or potato masher until almost smooth. Spoon into a lightly greased 13"x9" baking pan. Bake, uncovered, at 350 degrees for 45 minutes, or until potatoes are golden. Serves 8 to 10.

The crackle of a warm, cozy fire brings everyone together.
Enjoy a simple dinner of roasted hot dogs or toasty
pie-iron sandwiches, then make s'mores and
serve mugs of warm spiced cider.

Judy's Pot Roast & Gravy

Judy Bernacki
Henderson, NV

This roast is super-tender and makes its own tasty gravy.

3-lb. beef chuck or cross rib
   roast
2 10-3/4 oz. cans golden
   mushroom soup

1.35-oz. pkg. onion soup mix

Lightly spray a large sheet of aluminum foil with non-stick vegetable spray. Arrange roast on aluminum foil. Place in a 13"x9" baking pan coated with non-stick vegetable spray. Pour soup around roast; sprinkle soup mix on top. Wrap roast tightly with aluminum foil. Bake at 450 degrees 30 minutes; reduce temperature to 325 degrees and continue baking 3 hours. Serves 6 to 8.

Line a porch bench with pumpkins of all shapes and sizes. Hollow out some and tuck in a water-filled glass of cheery sunflowers, paint others and carve some to hold a glowing candle.

Roasted Chicken & Veggies

Leigh Ellen Eades
Summersville, WV

A friend first prepared this meal for my family during the holidays. On the drive home, my husband raved over its goodness. When we got home, I began playing with the ingredients myself until I came up with this recipe. This meal is such a hit in our home...there are never any leftovers!

2 T. olive oil
3 to 4-lb. chicken
4 carrots, cut in 2-inch pieces
4 to 5 potatoes, quartered
1/2 onion, quartered and
    separated into petals
14-1/2 oz. can chicken broth

1-1/4 c. white or purple grape
  juice
1/4 c. soy sauce
1 t. garlic, minced
1/2 t. dried parsley
1/2 t. dried thyme
salt and pepper to taste

Add oil to a saucepan over medium-high heat; brown chicken on all sides until golden. Transfer chicken to a greased roasting pan; surround with carrots and potatoes. In the same saucepan over medium heat, sauté onion until tender; set aside. Combine broth, grape juice and soy sauce; blend well. Stir in remaining ingredients; spoon over chicken. Top chicken with sautéed onion. Bake, covered, at 375 degrees for 48 minutes, basting occasionally. Uncover and continue to roast 12 additional minutes, until juices run clear when pierced. Serves 4.

Lengths of burlap are so easy to turn into a table runner...
simply cut and fringe the edges!

Broccoli Supreme

Linda Belon
Wintersville, OH

A delicious side that whips up in a jiffy!

1 egg, beaten
10-oz pkg. frozen chopped
   broccoli, partially thawed
8-1/2 oz. can creamed corn
1 T. onion, grated

1/4 t. salt
1/8 t. pepper
3 T. butter
1 c. herb-flavored stuffing mix

Combine egg, broccoli, corn, onion, salt and pepper. Melt butter
in a saucepan over medium heat. Add stuffing mix; toss to coat.
Stir 3/4 cup of stuffing mixture into vegetable mixture. Turn into
an ungreased 8"x8" baking pan. Sprinkle with remaining stuffing
mixture. Bake, uncovered, at 350 degrees for 35 to 40 minutes.
Makes 6 to 8 servings.

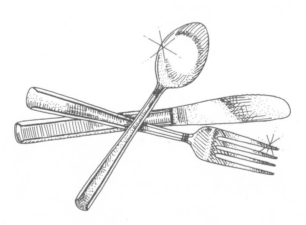

If your silverware needs polishing before the holidays,
try this quick & easy method for sparkling results. Line
a baking pan with aluminum foil, arrange silverware
over foil and sprinkle with baking soda to coat.
Cover with boiling water and let soak until
the tarnish is magically gone!

Southern Squash Casserole

Elizabeth Barnes
Princeton, KY

This recipe was a favorite in my husband's family,
until I made it for mine...now they love it too!

2 lbs. yellow squash, diced
salt and pepper to taste
1 onion, chopped
8-oz. container sour cream
10-3/4 oz. can cream of
    mushroom soup

Optional: 1 c. shredded
    Cheddar cheese
2 8-1/2 oz. pkgs. cornbread
    mix, prepared and crumbled

Season squash with salt and pepper. Place squash and onion in a saucepan; cover with water and bring to a boil. Cook over medium heat until tender; drain. Mash squash and onion slightly; stir in sour cream, soup and cheese, if desired. Fold 3/4 of the prepared cornbread into squash mixture; spread in a greased 13"x9" baking pan. Sprinkle remaining cornbread on top. Bake, uncovered, at 350 degrees until golden, about 25 minutes. Serves 8 to 10.

When family & friends come to visit, set out a book for them to sign. Little ones can even draw pictures inside. You can make it in no time...cover a plain journal with fabric, then add felted flowers, vintage buttons and rick rack.

Harvest Apple Salad

Melanie Johnston
Wilton, NH

I first tried this salad at a BBQ while I was expecting our son. It was a time in my life when I simply could not eat enough apples! One spoonful of the sweet freshness hits the spot.

8 Fuji apples, cored, peeled and
  chopped
32-oz. container plain yogurt

1/4 to 1/2 c. slivered almonds
1/4 to 1/2 c. sweetened dried
  cranberries

Combine apples and yogurt; stir in almonds and cranberries. Blend well. Refrigerate until ready to serve. Makes 8 servings.

Which apple is best? The tastiest pie apples are Rome, Jonathan, Fuji and Granny Smith. For salads, try McIntosh, Red Delicious, Empire and Gala.

Mom's Best-Ever Salad

Conni Butler
Castaic, CA

Mom always made this for our holiday dinners. Not only is it easy to prepare, it's so yummy too!

8-oz. pkg. cream cheese, softened
10 to 12 marshmallows
6-oz. pkg. lime gelatin mix
2 c. boiling water

2 c. cold water
1 c. crushed pineapple, drained
1 c. frozen whipped topping, thawed
Optional: 1/2 c. chopped nuts

In a large bowl, combine cream cheese, marshmallows and gelatin mix. Add boiling water; stir to dissolve. Stir in cold water; refrigerate until gelatin begins to thicken. Stir in drained pineapple, whipped topping and, if desired, chopped nuts. Spoon mixture into a 13"x9" pan or an 8-cup gelatin mold; refrigerate until firm. Makes 10 servings.

Cinnamon, pumpkin and apple pie-scented candles are perfect pairing with fall's crisp evenings. Make them last a bit longer…store them in the freezer until you're ready to burn them.

Gram's Stuffed Turkey Rolls

Vickie

Both of my favorite Thanksgiving flavors rolled into one!

4 slices turkey breast, sliced
   1/2-inch thick
2 to 3 t. all-purpose flour
1 T. butter

1/4 c. dry red wine or beef
   broth
3/4 c. chicken broth

Place turkey slices between 2 sheets of wax paper. Use a meat mallet to flatten until 1/4-inch thick. Arrange turkey slices on a work surface; spoon 1/4 of Sausage Stuffing onto the center of each slice. Roll and secure with toothpicks. Coat rolls lightly with flour; set aside. Melt butter in a large skillet, add turkey rolls and brown on all sides. Remove turkey from skillet; set aside and keep warm. Pour wine or beef broth into skillet and cook over medium heat about 5 minutes, scraping up browned bits. Stir in chicken broth, then arrange turkey rolls in skillet. Cook, covered, over low heat 8 to 10 minutes. Serve with gravy from skillet. Makes 4 servings.

Sausage Stuffing:

1 T. butter
2 T. onion, minced
1 clove garlic, minced
1/4 lb. mild ground pork
   sausage
1/4 t. dried sage

1/4 t. red pepper flakes
1/4 t. dried thyme
2 slices day-old bread,
   crumbled
salt and pepper to taste

Heat butter in a skillet over medium heat. Stir in onion and garlic; sauté until tender. Add sausage, breaking up with fork; cook until browned. Do not drain. Reduce heat to low; stir in remaining ingredients. Cook 5 minutes to blend flavors.

Green Beans Almondine

Michelle Campen
Peoria, IL

*I just love green beans and I'm always looking for new ways
to prepare them. This recipe is a new favorite.*

2 lbs. green beans, trimmed
   and halved
8 slices bacon, chopped
2 cloves garlic, thinly sliced

1 t. Italian seasoning
1 c. sliced almonds
1 t. soy sauce

Place beans in a stockpot of salted boiling water and cook for
2 minutes. Drain and run under cold water. Drain again. Set aside
to dry on paper towels. Cook bacon in a large, heavy skillet over
medium-high heat until crisp. Drain all but 2 tablespoons of
drippings from skillet. Add garlic, seasoning and almonds to skillet;
sauté one minute. Stir in beans and sauté until beans are crisp-
tender. Drizzle soy sauce over beans; stir and serve immediately.
Serves 8.

Turn a basket of green beans from the fall farmers' market
into a slow-cooker side for dinner. It couldn't be easier!
Combine 2 pounds trimmed beans with 2 tablespoons oil,
one diced onion, 6 slices chopped bacon and 3/4 cup
water; add salt and pepper to taste. Cover and cook
on high setting for 4 to 5 hours.

Nellie's Spinach Salad

Denise Webb
Galveston, IN

My friend Nellie serves this delicious salad and it's become one of my favorites!

6-oz. pkg. baby spinach
6 slices bacon, crisply cooked
   and crumbled
1 onion, chopped
1/2 c. sliced mushrooms
4-oz. container crumbled
   feta cheese
1 avocado, peeled, pitted
   and sliced

1/3 c. oil
2 T. sugar
1/4 t. mustard
3 T. vinegar
1/2 t. salt
1 T. onion, grated

In a large bowl, toss together spinach, bacon, onion, mushrooms, cheese and avocado. Combine remaining ingredients in a jar with a tight-fitting lid; shake well to combine. Pour dressing over salad; toss and serve. Serves 4 to 6.

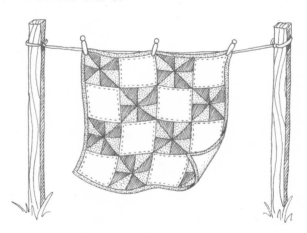

When Indian summer rolls around, it's time to freshen up quilts...cool, crisp nights will be here soon! After a gentle washing, air-dry quilts on the clothesline. The warm sun and gentle breezes will make them smell oh-so sweet.

Grandma's Wilted Lettuce

Jenna Fowls
Warsaw, OH

My grandma used to make this recipe for every holiday. Now, I have the pleasure of making it for special occasions...it's one of my favorite salads. To save time, I usually heat the water, vinegar, sugar, and drippings in a mug in the microwave.

2 heads leaf lettuce, torn
Optional: 1/8 t. salt, 1/8 t.
   pepper
2 eggs, hard-boiled, peeled and
   quartered
Optional: 2 green onions, sliced

4 to 6 slices bacon, crisply
   cooked and crumbled,
   drippings reserved
2 T. water
1/4 c. vinegar
1 T. sugar

Arrange lettuce in a serving bowl; season with salt and pepper if desired. Add eggs and onions, if using. Toss to combine; top with crumbled bacon. Combine remaining ingredients and drippings in a saucepan. Heat to boiling; pour over salad. Toss again and serve immediately. Makes 6 servings.

Tie up bunches of herbs to dry and hang them in your kitchen. They'll add the freshest taste to those simmering soups & stews and wonderful comfort foods you'll be making all harvest season long.

Tilapia with Dill Sauce

Lori Rosenberg
University Heights, OH

This dish is one my family loves and requests often.

1 lb. tilapia fillets	1/2 c. sour cream
salt and pepper to taste	1/8 t. garlic powder
1/2 to 1 T. Cajun seasoning	1 t. lemon juice
1 lemon, thinly sliced	2 T. fresh dill, chopped
1/4 c. mayonnaise	

Sprinkle both sides of fillets with salt, pepper and seasoning. Arrange fillets in a single layer in a lightly greased 13"x9" baking pan. Arrange 2 lemon slices over each fillet. Bake, uncovered, at 350 degrees for 15 to 20 minutes, or until fish flakes easily with a fork. Blend remaining ingredients in a small bowl; serve with baked fish. Serves 4.

Sit in front of a cozy fire and stitch up some handmade gifts for friends & family. They'll treasure a sweet little sachet filled with dried lavender, squares of felted wool for coasters, or an embroidered tea towel.

Savory Suppers

Potato Latkes

Debbie Muer
Encino, CA

I like to serve these potato pancakes with a salad for a complete meal.

2 c. potatoes, peeled and grated
2 eggs, beaten
1/8 t. baking powder
1-1/2 t. salt
1 T. all-purpose flour or
    matzo meal

1/8 t. pepper
oil for frying
Garnish: sour cream or
    applesauce

Mix all ingredients except oil and garnish together. Heat oil in a skillet over medium-high heat. Pour about one tablespoon of batter for each pancake into hot oil and fry until golden. Top with a dollop of sour cream or applesauce. Serves 4 to 6.

Turkey Potato Pancakes

Kathi Duerr
Fulda, MN

I don't remember how I discovered this recipe, but I do know that it became an instant Duerr family favorite!

3 eggs, beaten
3 c. potatoes, peeled and
    shredded
1-1/2 c. cooked turkey, finely
    chopped

1/4 c. green onion, sliced
2 T. all-purpose flour
1-1/2 t. salt
oil for frying
Optional: cranberry sauce

Combine eggs, potatoes, turkey, onion, flour and salt; mix well. Heat about 1/4-inch oil in a large skillet over medium-high heat. Pour batter by 1/3 cupfuls into hot oil. Fry 5 to 6 minutes on each side, or until potatoes are tender and pancakes are golden. Serve with cranberry sauce, if desired. Makes 1 dozen pancakes.

Mother's Pork Chops & Apples

Barbara Encababian
Easton, PA

This recipe is wonderful when the weather is cold. The oven warms the kitchen, the smells are fabulous and the flavors all blend together.

2 T. oil
6 pork chops
3 to 4 apples, cored and sliced

1/4 c. brown sugar, packed
1/2 t. cinnamon
2 T. butter

Heat oil in a skillet over medium-high heat; brown pork chops on both sides. Place unpeeled apple slices in a greased 13"x9" baking pan. Sprinkle with brown sugar and cinnamon; dot with butter. Arrange pork chops on top. Cover and bake at 350 degrees for 1-1/2 hours. Serves 6.

Candied Pecan Carrots

Nicole Manley
Great Lakes, IL

I created this recipe when I was trying to get my son and my husband to eat their veggies. They aren't too fond of carrots, but this is one dish they don't pass up!

1/4 c. butter
5 T. brown sugar, packed
1 t. nutmeg
2 t. cinnamon

1/4 c. chopped pecans
16-oz. pkg. frozen carrots, cooked

Melt butter in a saucepan over medium heat; stir in brown sugar. Stir until dissolved. Add remaining ingredients except carrots; stir well. Combine brown sugar mixture and cooked carrots in an ungreased 2-1/2 quart casserole dish. Bake, uncovered, at 350 degrees for 15 to 20 minutes. Makes 4 to 6 servings.

Sweet Potato Casserole

Jackie Hatfield
Shepherdsville, KY

This is the first dish that my son goes for!

2 c. sweet potatoes, cooked
   and mashed
1-1/2 c. sugar
1 c. milk
2 eggs, beaten
1/2 t. cinnamon
1/2 t. nutmeg

1/2 t. pumpkin pie spice
1 c. corn flake cereal, crushed
1/2 c. chopped pecans
3/4 c. butter, melted
1/2 c. brown sugar, packed
1 c. mini marshmallows

Mix sweet potatoes, sugar, milk, eggs and spices. Spoon into a one-quart casserole dish sprayed with non-stick vegetable spray. Bake, covered, at 350 degrees for 30 to 40 minutes. Toss together cereal, pecans, butter and brown sugar. Sprinkle over sweet potato mixture. Return to oven and bake, uncovered, an additional 10 minutes. Sprinkle marshmallows on top and continue baking, uncovered, until marshmallows melt. Serves 8 to 10.

At the next barn sale, look for a roomy vintage mixing bowl. Fill it with all varieties of deliciously crisp apples from the orchard. What a perfect centerpiece for your kitchen table!

Cranberry Chicken

Lisa Robason
Corpus Christi, TX

This is a family-favorite, quick-fix recipe for busy holiday evenings.

8-oz. can whole-berry
   cranberry sauce
1 c. French salad dressing
1.35-oz. pkg. onion soup mix
8 boneless, skinless chicken
   breasts

1/4 t. pepper
4 c. cooked rice
Optional: fresh parsley,
   chopped

Combine cranberry sauce, salad dressing and soup mix. Spread
half of the cranberry mixture into a greased 13"x9" baking pan.
Arrange chicken in a single layer over sauce mixture; season with
pepper, then top with remaining cranberry mixture. Bake, covered,
at 325 degrees for 35 to 45 minutes, or until juices run clear when
chicken is pierced. Serve over cooked rice and garnish with parsley,
if desired. Serves 8.

Make a trip to the farmers' market for the freshest
fall fruits. Turned into jams & jellies, they'll be
oh-so welcome gifts throughout the year.

Chicken Tarragon

Claudia Passaro
Chester, NJ

A special-event dinner in our family.

2 lbs. boneless, skinless
    chicken breasts
1 c. Italian-flavored dry
    bread crumbs
1 T. vegetable oil
1 T. olive oil
3 cloves garlic, minced

2 T. butter
dried oregano, salt and pepper
    to taste
1/2 c. tarragon vinegar
14-oz. can artichoke hearts,
    quartered and juice reserved

Coat chicken breasts with bread crumbs. Add oils to a skillet; brown chicken over medium heat until juices run clear. Remove chicken from pan and cut into bite-size pieces. To the same skillet, add remaining ingredients except artichokes. Stir and cook over medium heat, 3 to 4 minutes. Add artichokes with juice. Heat through and pour over chicken. Serves 6 to 8.

When leaves start to turn, cozy-up your outdoor
furniture with flannel or fleece pillows.

Meggie's Ratatouille

Tori Willis
Champaign, IL

*When my friend Meggie served this dish at a harvest get-together,
I couldn't get enough. I had to have the recipe before I left!*

1 eggplant, peeled and cut into
  1-inch cubes
1 onion, diced
1 red pepper, diced
1 zucchini, cut into 1-inch
  cubes

1/4 c. sun-dried tomato salad
  dressing
14-1/2 oz. can diced tomatoes
1/4 c. grated Parmesan cheese
1 c. shredded mozzarella
  cheese

Sauté vegetables with salad dressing in a large oven-proof skillet
over medium heat. Add tomatoes with juice; cook for 15 minutes.
Sprinkle with cheeses. Bake, uncovered, at 350 degrees for
15 minutes. Serves 6 to 8.

Fill your harvest buffet with something unexpected.
Hollow out a loaf of sourdough bread for a bowl and
fill it with all those savory olives found at the deli.
Serve dips with vegetable chips…they can be found in
fall colors like orange, red and gold!

Slow-Cooker Veggie Lasagna

Cathy Estes
Larned, KS

*This is always requested when fresh veggies are plentiful...
it's a really scrumptious all-veggie dish.*

1-1/2 c. shredded mozzarella
   cheese
1/2 c. cottage cheese
1/3 c. grated Parmesan cheese
1 egg, beaten
1 t. dried oregano
1/4 t. garlic powder
16-oz. jar marinara sauce

1-1/4 c. zucchini, diced
   and divided
8 no-boil lasagna noodles
6-oz. pkg. baby spinach,
   divided
1 c. sliced mushrooms, divided
Optional: fresh basil, chopped

Spray a slow cooker with non-stick vegetable spray. In a bowl,
mix together cheeses, egg, oregano and garlic powder. Spread
2 to 3 tablespoons marinara sauce in the bottom of slow cooker.
Sprinkle half the zucchini over sauce, top with 1/3 of the cheese
mixture. Break 2 noodles into pieces and cover cheese. Spread
2 to 3 tablespoons more sauce over noodles; layer half the spinach
and half the mushrooms. Repeat layering, ending with cheese
mixture and remaining sauce. Firmly press ingredients into slow
cooker. Cover and cook on low setting 4 to 5 hours. Allow lasagna
to stand 20 minutes before serving. If desired, garnish with basil.
Serves 8.

Host a slow-cooker supper to celebrate harvest season!
Invite friends to bring their favorite slow-cooker dishes,
from mains to desserts. After dinner, take a hayride,
carve pumpkins or have a scarecrow-building contest.
It's all about being together and making memories.

Upside-Down Roast Turkey

Emily Puskac
New Cumberland, WV

The secret to this juicy turkey? Baking it upside-down!

18-lb. turkey
14-oz. can chicken broth
3/4 c. butter, divided
1 clove garlic, minced
1 t. salt
1/2 t. pepper

1 t. dried basil
1/4 t. dried rosemary
1/4 t. dried thyme
1/4 t. dried marjoram
1 c. dry white wine or
   chicken broth

Pat turkey dry with paper towels; set aside. Pour broth into roasting pan. Insert roasting rack in the bottom of pan; coat rack with butter. Rub 1/4 cup butter over turkey. Combine garlic, salt, pepper and herbs; sprinkle evenly over turkey. Place turkey upside-down on rack; bake, uncovered, at 325 degrees for 40 minutes. Meanwhile, melt remaining butter in a saucepan over medium heat; stir in wine or broth. Baste turkey after 40 minutes, then baste every 30 minutes. After turkey has roasted 3-1/4 hours, remove roasting pan from oven and carefully turn turkey breast-side up. Return to oven and continue baking one additional hour, or until an instant-read meat thermometer registers 165 degrees at the thickest part of the thigh. Let rest for 20 minutes before carving. Serves 10.

Keep this chart handy when it's time to thaw your
holiday turkey in the refrigerator:
12 to 16 pounds will take 3 to 4 days
16 to 20 pounds will take 4 to 5 days
20 to 24 pounds will take 5 to 6 days

Mom's Best Stuffing

Kimberly Pfleiderer
Galion, OH

*This is the recipe Mom makes every Thanksgiving and Christmas.
The house smells wonderful while it's baking.*

2 cubes chicken boullion
2 c. boiling water
2 loaves bread, torn
1 c. butter, melted and slightly
   cooled

4 eggs, beaten
2 onions, finely chopped
2-1/2 t. dried sage
2 stalks celery, finely chopped

Dissolve boullion cubes in water to make a broth; set aside. Place
bread in a large bowl; pour butter and eggs over bread to moisten.
Add remaining ingredients; toss gently. Add only enough broth
to moisten bread to desired consistency. If stuffing a turkey, use
3/4 cup stuffing for each pound of turkey; loosely fill cavity and
roast turkey as desired. To bake in a casserole dish, spoon stuffing
mixture into a buttered 1-1/2 quart casserole dish. Bake, covered,
at 325 degrees for 45 minutes to one hour. Serves 10 to 12.

Try this sweet-hot butter for spreading over homemade
cornbread...delicious alongside a bowl of chili! Blend
together one cup softened butter with 1/4 cup maple syrup
and 1/2 teaspoon Mexican hot pepper sauce.

Italian Tossed Salad

Janice Woods
Northern Cambria, PA

A favorite recipe I make for home as well as get-togethers. The dressing is terrific, not only on this salad, but drizzled over hoagies and as a marinade for chicken as well.

12-oz. pkg. salad greens
1 c. shredded mozzarella
   cheese
1 c. canned kidney beans,
   drained and rinsed

1 c. pepperoni, diced
1/4 c. onion, chopped
1/2 green pepper, chopped
2 tomatoes, diced

In a salad bowl, combine all ingredients; drizzle with Great Italian Salad Dressing. Toss to coat. Serves 4 to 6.

Great Italian Salad Dressing:

1.05-oz. env. Italian salad
   dressing mix
1/3 c. sugar
3 cloves garlic, minced

3/4 c. cider vinegar
3/4 c. water
3/4 c. oil

In a quart jar, combine all ingredients. Tighten lid; shake to combine. Store in refrigerator until chilled. Shake again to blend before serving. Makes about 2-1/3 cups.

Try a natural theme for your harvest table…use items found in your own backyard. A colorful, leafy branch can be a clever placecard when you tie on a name tag.

Marilyn's Spaghetti Salad

*Marilyn Morel
Keene, NH*

This is a great dish to take to gatherings or to potlucks. I first had this dish almost 10 years ago and it's still one of my favorites!

16-oz. pkg. spaghetti,
  uncooked
2 cucumbers, peeled, seeded
  and diced
2 tomatoes, diced
3 green onions, chopped

1/2 green pepper, diced
1/2 red pepper, diced
8-oz. bottle sun-dried tomato
  vinaigrette salad dressing
salt and pepper to taste

Cook pasta according to package directions; drain and rinse with cold water. In a large bowl, combine pasta with remaining ingredients except salt and pepper. Toss well to coat. Refrigerate several hours or overnight before serving. Season with salt and pepper just before serving. Serves 6.

Decorate a plain white pumpkin in no time at all.
A stencil and a bit of black paint is all it takes. Show off
your pumpkin by setting it on a footed cake stand.

24-Hour Fruit Salad

Cindy Neel
Gooseberry Patch

*I made this for our Wednesday Salad Bar luncheon here at
Gooseberry Patch. It's really tart and lemony.*

2 20-oz. cans pineapple
chunks, drained and juice
reserved
6-oz. can frozen orange juice
concentrate
3.4-oz. pkg. instant lemon
pudding mix
3 bananas, sliced

2 15-1/4 oz. cans pears,
drained and diced
2 15-1/4 oz. cans apricots,
drained and diced
2 15-1/4 oz. cans peaches,
drained and diced
15-oz. can mandarin oranges,
drained

Pour reserved pineapple juice in a bowl. Stir in orange juice
concentrate and pudding mix; stir to dissolve. Add pineapple,
bananas, pears, apricots, peaches and oranges. Mix well and
refrigerate 24 hours. Makes 16 servings.

Dress up fabric napkins in no time. Roll each napkin,
tie with ribbon in russet or rich brown, and tuck a
pair of acorns under the ribbon.

Frozen Cranberry Salad

Carleen Pettit
Sidney, OH

*This is a special salad we've enjoyed for Thanksgiving dinner
for years. It's so good with turkey.*

16-oz. can jellied cranberry
   sauce
1 t. lemon juice
1 c. whipping cream
8-oz. pkg. cream cheese,
   softened

1/4 c. powdered sugar
3/4 c. chopped pecans
1 T. mayonnaise or
   mayonnaise-style salad
   dressing

Blend cranberry sauce and lemon juice; pour into a 1-1/2 quart
casserole dish. Using an electric mixer with chilled beaters, beat
whipping cream on high speed until soft peaks form. Fold in
remaining ingredients. Layer mixture over cranberry sauce; freeze.
Serves 10.

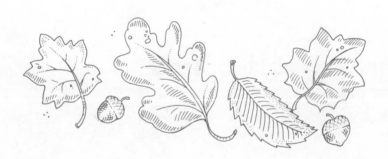

The easiest cranberry sauce ever! Combine one pound
cranberries, one cup sugar and 1/2 cup water. Stir in the
zest of 2 oranges, and then the oranges, chopped. Place
in a saucepan and cook over low heat, covered, for
3 hours, stirring occasionally. Refrigerate until chilled.

Family Favorite Corn Soufflé

Donna Maltman
Toledo, OH

An absolute must-have for Thanksgiving dinner.

15-oz. can corn, drained
8-1/2 oz. pkg. cornbread mix
14-3/4 oz. can creamed corn
1 c. sour cream

1/4 c. butter, melted
8-oz. pkg. shredded Cheddar
cheese

Combine all ingredients except cheese. Pour into a lightly greased 13"x9" glass baking pan. Cover with aluminum foil. Bake at 350 degrees for 30 minutes. Uncover and add cheese. Return to oven and continue baking until cheese is bubbly and golden, about 15 minutes. Serves 12 to 14.

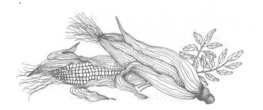

Honey-Glazed Ham Steaks

Kristin Pittis
Dennison, OH

With only 3 ingredients, this makes a great quick dinner. I like to serve it with scalloped potatoes and a crisp green salad.

1/4 c. brown sugar, packed
2 T. honey

4 ham steaks

Combine brown sugar and honey in a plastic zipping bag. Add ham steaks; seal bag and rub sugar mixture into ham. Refrigerate 30 minutes. Remove ham from bag and grill over medium heat, 2 to 3 minutes per side. Makes 4 servings.

Party Potatoes

Mary Patenaude
Griswold, CT

These are the yummiest potatoes ever!

4 c. mashed potatoes
1 c. sour cream
8-oz. pkg. cream cheese,
  softened
1 t. dried chives

1/4 t. garlic powder
1/4 c. dry bread crumbs
1 T. butter, melted
1/2 c. shredded Cheddar cheese

In a large bowl, combine potatoes, sour cream, cream cheese, chives and garlic powder. Turn into a greased 2-quart casserole dish. Combine bread crumbs with butter; sprinkle over potatoes. Bake, uncovered, at 350 degrees for 50 to 60 minutes. Top with Cheddar cheese and serve. Serves 8 to 10.

If you're baking potatoes for dinner tonight, make them even tastier by rubbing the skin with softened butter and salting them before baking!

Best-Ever Cheddar Burgers

Jo Ann

All the yummy flavors that go into this recipe make for one fantastic-tasting burger!

2 lbs. ground turkey
4 green onions, finely chopped
1/3 c. fresh parsley, chopped
1 T. grill seasoning
1 t. poultry seasoning
2 T. oil
1 Granny Smith apple, cored
   and thinly sliced

8 slices Cheddar cheese
1/4 c. whole-berry cranberry
   sauce
2 T. spicy brown mustard
4 buns, split and toasted
8 leaves green leaf lettuce

Combine turkey, onions, parsley and seasonings; form into 4 patties. Heat oil in a skillet over medium-high heat. Add patties and cook 5 minutes per side, or until desired doneness is reached. Arrange 2 to 3 apple slices and 2 cheese slices over each patty. Remove skillet from heat; cover to let cheese melt. Blend cranberry sauce and mustard together; spread on cut sides of buns. Add lettuce and burgers; close sandwiches. Serves 4.

Warm up beds on chilly autumn nights with flannel sheets, a cozy quilt and plump feather pillows...ahhh.

Surprise Fries

Teresa Podracky
Solon, OH

My kids love these with burgers and brats.

2-lb. butternut squash, halved
   lengthwise, seeded and
   peeled
2 t. olive oil
salt to taste

1/2 t. ground cumin
1/2 t. chili powder
1/2 c. sour cream
2 T. maple syrup

Cut squash halves to resemble French fries; slice about 1/2-inch wide and 3 inches long. Add oil to a large bowl; add squash, tossing to coat. Line a baking sheet with aluminum foil; spray with non-stick vegetable spray. Arrange slices in a single layer on top. Bake at 425 degrees for 35 minutes, or until tender. Combine salt, cumin and chili powder; sprinkle desired amount over fries. Blend together sour cream and syrup as a dipping sauce. Serves 4.

Call a girlfriend and take a knitting class together.
Soon you'll be making cozy mittens and snuggly socks,
and oh, the fun you'll have!

Maple-Marinated Salmon

Joan White
Malvern, PA

*The flavors of ginger and maple combine to bring out
the best in the salmon.*

3/4 c. maple syrup
2 T. fresh ginger, peeled
   and grated
2 T. lemon juice
2 T. low-sodium soy sauce

1/2 t. pepper
1/4 t. salt
2-1/4 lbs. skin-on salmon
   fillets

In a greased 13"x9" baking pan, stir together all ingredients
except salmon. Place salmon, skin-side up, in pan. Cover and
refrigerate 15 minutes. Turn; marinate another 15 minutes. Line a
separate 13"x9" baking pan with parchment paper. Place salmon
on parchment, skin-side down; brush with marinade. Bake at
400 degrees for 10 minutes. Brush with remaining marinade and
return to oven for 10 to 15 minutes, until fish flakes easily with
a fork. Discard skin before serving. Serves 6.

Cooler fall weather makes it the best time for a backyard
campout. Cook over a fire, tell stories, make shadow
puppets, play charades, and then curl up in a
cozy quilt under a harvest moon.

Autumn Apple-Cheddar Chicken
Sarah Cameron
Maryville, TN

This is an awesome, heartwarming fall dish that's savory and sweet. Serve with fresh carrots and broccoli and you have a meal the whole family will love.

5 to 6 boneless, skinless
  chicken breasts
2 sleeves round buttery
  crackers, crushed
1/2 c. plus 3 T. butter, melted
1/4 c. all-purpose flour

3/4 c. milk
10-3/4 oz. can Cheddar cheese
  soup
1 c. shredded Cheddar cheese
3 Golden Delicious apples,
  cored and sliced

Place chicken in a large pot of boiling water. Cook for 8 to 10 minutes; set aside. Combine crumbs with 1/2 cup butter; mix thoroughly. Add remaining butter to a saucepan; stir in flour and cook about one minute, stirring often. Add milk, soup and cheese; stir to blend until cheese is melted. Place chicken in a greased 13"x9" baking pan. Cover chicken with cheese sauce, top with sliced apples and sprinkle with cracker mixture. Bake, covered, at 350 degrees for 35 to 40 minutes. Makes 6 servings.

Use oversize mugs in an unexpected way…they're just the right size for servings of steamy soups and stews, and the handle makes them so easy to hold onto.

Italian-Style Pot Roast

Rosemary Kerns
St. Joseph, MO

My kids love this roast, and the slow cooker makes it so simple.

1 onion, sliced
3 cloves garlic, minced
28-oz. can crushed tomatoes
2 T. balsamic vinegar
1 T. Worcestershire sauce

1 T. Italian seasoning
2 t. brown sugar, packed
salt and pepper to taste
2 to 3-lb. beef chuck roast

Blend together all ingredients except roast in a bowl. Pour half the mixture into a slow cooker and add roast; pour remaining mixture over top. Cover and cook on low setting for 6 to 8 hours. Serves 6.

Sew a blanket stitch around the edges of a vintage
tea towel to make a basket liner...what a pretty way
to keep rolls warm throughout dinner!

COZY

Desserts

Warm Fall Lemon Cake

Tonya Lewis-Holm
Scottsburg, IN

After a leisurely fall meal, my family loves lingering over dessert...
especially one that warms them from head to toe. This favorite recipe
comes together in no time and never fails to impress. If you
are a real lemon lover, try adding one tablespoon lemon zest and
2 tablespoons of freshly squeezed lemon juice to the pudding mixes.

18-1/2 oz. pkg. yellow cake
  mix
2 c. milk
1-1/4 c. water

2 3.4-oz. pkgs. instant lemon
  pudding mix
1/3 c. sugar
Garnish: 2 T. powdered sugar

Prepare cake batter as directed on package; pour into a greased
13"x9" baking pan. Set aside. Pour milk and water into a large
bowl; stir in dry pudding mixes and sugar. Beat with a wire whisk
for 2 minutes, or until well blended. Pour milk mixture into baking
pan over cake batter; do not stir. Place baking pan on a baking sheet
to catch any bubble-overs. Bake at 350 degrees for 55 minutes to
one hour, or until a toothpick inserted near the center comes out
clean. Cool for 20 minutes to allow sauce to thicken. Dust with
powdered sugar. Store leftovers in the refrigerator. Serves 16.

When making caramel apples, give them a quick
sprinkle with fall-themed jimmies and sprinkles
while the caramel is still warm...so festive!

Cherry-Chocolate Yum Cake

Christine Takada
Farmington, MN

I came up with this dessert one night when my grown children and their families came for dinner. It gets gobbled up immediately and everyone I've ever made it for says it's delicious!

18-1/2 oz. pkg. chocolate cake mix

21-oz. can cherry pie filling
12-oz. can chocolate frosting

Prepare cake batter according to package directions; pour half the batter into a well-greased Bundt® pan. Spoon 2/3 of pie filling on top of batter; pull a butter knife through pie filling to swirl into batter. Top with remaining batter. Bake cake according to package directions, testing with a toothpick for doneness. Remove from oven and let cake stand for 10 minutes. Place a large plate over bottom of pan and invert onto plate. Let cool completely. Just before serving, microwave chocolate frosting according to can directions. Pour frosting over cake, then pour remaining pie filling over frosting. Let stand 5 minutes before slicing. Serves 10 to 12.

Besides greasing and flouring a Bundt® pan, here's another tip to help the cake slip out of the pan easily. Just before the cake is done baking, lay a folded bath towel in the sink and soak with very hot water. When the cake comes out of the oven, immediately set it on the towel, pan-side down, for 10 seconds. Invert the pan onto a wire rack or cake plate to allow the cake to cool completely.

Cookie Dough Brownies

Linda Vogt
Las Vegas, NV

You will definitely get your chocolate fix
with this one...it's simply decadent!

2 c. sugar
1/2 c. baking cocoa
1 c. oil
2 t. vanilla extract
1-1/2 c. all-purpose flour
1/2 t. salt
4 eggs, beaten

Optional: 1/2 c. chopped
 walnuts
1 c. semi-sweet chocolate chips
1 T. shortening
Garnish: 1/4 c. chopped
 walnuts

Mix all ingredients together except chocolate chips, shortening and garnish. Pour into a greased 13"x9" baking pan and bake at 350 degrees for 30 minutes. Cool completely. Prepare Cookie Dough and spread over cooled brownies. Add chocolate chips to a microwave-safe bowl and melt on low. Add shortening, stirring to blend. Drizzle over brownies. Garnish with nuts. Refrigerate until glaze is firm. Makes 8 to 12 servings.

Cookie Dough:

1/2 c. butter, softened
1/4 c. sugar
1 t. vanilla extract

1/2 c. brown sugar, packed
2 T. milk
1 c. all-purpose flour

Mix together all ingredients in a small bowl.

After dinner, enjoy some
Halloween storytelling
outside around a fire or
inside by candlelight...
frightfully fun!

Cozy Desserts

Autumn Caramel Corn

Jennifer Lemon
Lexington, OH

Every fall, I make this caramel corn to enjoy after we go apple picking. We enjoy it so much, it's become a family tradition.

1 c. brown sugar, packed
1/4 c. dark corn syrup
1/2 c. butter
1/2 t. salt

1/2 t. vanilla extract
1/4 t. baking soda
3 qts. popped popcorn

Combine brown sugar, corn syrup, butter and salt in a saucepan. Bring to a boil over medium-high heat, cook for 5 minutes. Stir in vanilla and baking soda. Place popcorn in a very large bowl; pour brown sugar mixture over popcorn and toss to coat. Spoon into a buttered 15"x10" jelly-roll pan. Bake at 250 degrees for one hour, stirring every 15 minutes. Makes 3 quarts.

Brandon's Pumpkin Squares

Beth Bundy
Long Prairie, MN

My son Brandon loves anything with pumpkin in it...he requests this dessert all year 'round! His love for these bars makes them very special to me.

12-oz. can evaporated milk
3 eggs, beaten
2 t. pumpkin pie spice
1/2 t. salt
1 c. sugar

15-oz. can pumpkin
18-1/2 oz. pkg. yellow cake
   mix
1/2 c. butter, sliced
Garnish: whipped topping

Combine all ingredients except cake mix, butter and garnish. Pour into a greased 13"x11" pan. Sprinkle on dry cake mix; do not stir. Dot with butter. Bake at 350 degrees for 30 to 35 minutes. Serve with whipped topping. Makes 20 squares.

Chocolate Icebox Pie

Margaret McNeil
Germantown, TN

If you'd like, top servings with a dollop of whipped cream,
a sprinkle of baking cocoa and some chocolate curls.

2/3 c. milk
3/4 c. semi-sweet chocolate
   chips
2 T. cornstarch
1/4 c. cold water
14-oz. can sweetened
   condensed milk

3 eggs, beaten
1 t. vanilla extract
3 T. butter
8-inch chocolate cookie crust

Pour milk into a 3-quart saucepan over medium heat. Heat just until milk begins to bubble around the edges. Do not boil. Remove from heat and whisk in chocolate chips until melted. Cool slightly. Stir cornstarch into cold water until dissolved. Whisk cornstarch mixture, sweetened condensed milk, eggs and vanilla into chocolate mixture. Bring to a boil over medium heat, whisking constantly. Boil one minute or until mixture thickens and is smooth; do not overcook. Remove from heat and whisk in butter. Spoon mixture into pie crust. Cover and chill 8 hours. Makes 8 servings.

Top a favorite pie with a chocolate-licorice spider web! Arrange six, 4-inch pieces of licorice in a star shape on a sheet of parchment paper. Place melting chocolate in a plastic zipping bag and heat in a microwave until soft. Snip off one corner and drizzle over licorice in a web shape. Add a large dot of chocolate in the center to "glue" the web together.

Amish Sugar Cream Pie

Debra Manley
Bowling Green, OH

This is the best-tasting sugar cream pie I have ever had! A great change from the traditional pumpkin at Thanksgiving.

3/4 c. sugar
1/2 t. salt
2-1/2 c. half-and-half
1/4 c. brown sugar, packed
1/4 c. cornstarch

1/2 c. butter, sliced
1 t. vanilla extract
10-inch pie crust, baked
Garnish: cinnamon

Mix sugar, salt and half-and-half in a saucepan over medium heat. Bring mixture just to a boil, until frothy. Stir occasionally. In another saucepan, combine brown sugar and cornstarch, whisking until smooth. Gradually whisk in hot half-and-half mixture until smooth. Add butter and return to heat. Cook, whisking constantly, until thick and mixture bubbles up in center. Add vanilla; stir. Pour into crust and sprinkle with cinnamon. Bake at 325 degrees for 20 minutes, or until pie is golden on top. Filling will be loose when removed from oven, but will firm up as pie cools. Cool completely. Serves 10 to 12.

Dress up a pie crust with pretty scallops. Simply press two sizes of measuring spoons along the pie crust edge before baking.

Harvest-Time Apple Squares

Beth Bundy
Long Prairie, MN

Always an autumn favorite at our house.

2 c. all-purpose flour
1 c. brown sugar, packed
3/4 c. sugar, divided
1-1/2 t. cinnamon
1/2 c. butter, softened
1 c. chopped walnuts
8-oz. pkg. cream cheese,
   softened

2 T. milk
1 egg, beaten
1/2 t. vanilla extract
3-1/2 c. Granny Smith apples,
   cored, peeled and chopped

Combine flour, brown sugar, 1/2 cup sugar and cinnamon. Cut
in butter until mixture resembles coarse crumbs; stir in walnuts.
Reserve 2 cups crumb mixture. Press remaining mixture into a
greased 13"x9" baking pan. Combine cream cheese and milk,
mixing until well blended. Add remaining sugar, egg and vanilla.
Mix well and pour over crust. Top with apples. Sprinkle with
reserved crumb mixture. Bake at 350 degrees for 30 minutes.
Cool before cutting. Makes one dozen squares.

An artist's paintbrush and black acrylic paint are all you
need to add a written welcome to your pumpkins. Paint on
"Welcome Friends" or paint several pumpkins for an eerie
Halloween greeting such as, "I'd turn back if I were you!"

Cynthia's Banana-Oatmeal Cookies
*Cynthia Dodge
Layton, UT*

*This cookie recipe came together when my children were very young.
They didn't like banana bread, but they devoured these cookies!
Everyone asks for the recipe after they have tried one. Once you take
a bite, you'll love them too!*

3/4 c. margarine
1 c. sugar
1 egg, beaten
1/2 t. banana extract
1/4 c. wheat germ
4 to 5 bananas, sliced
2 to 2-1/2 c. quick-cooking
   oats, uncooked

1/8 t. cinnamon
1/8 t. nutmeg
1-1/2 c. all-purpose flour
1/2 t. baking soda
1/4 t. salt
Optional: 1 c. water, 1/2 to
   3/4 c. raisins, 12-oz. can
   vanilla frosting

Beat margarine and sugar together with an electric mixer on
medium speed. Add egg and extract; blend well. Add wheat germ;
blend. Stir in bananas, 2 cups oats, cinnamon and nutmeg; blend
well. Whisk together flour, baking soda and salt; stir into dough. Add
additional 1/2 cup oats if dough appears too thin. If adding raisins,
soak raisins in one cup of water for one minute; drain well and add
to dough. Drop dough by teaspoonfuls onto parchment paper-lined
baking sheets. Bake at 400 degrees for 11 to 13 minutes. If frosting
is desired, spoon frosting into a microwave-safe bowl. Microwave
about 30 seconds, or until very thin; stir. Dip tops of cookies
into frosting; set aside to cool. Refrigerate any leftovers. Makes
4 dozen cookies.

Dress up a Halloween dessert table with sweets
stacked on black hobnail cake stands, bowls of black
jellybeans or jars of black licorice sticks. Scatter colorful
dried leaves on the table and let everyone enjoy!

Turtle Pumpkin Pie

Tonya Lewis-Holm
Scottsburg, IN

*I made this wonderful pie during the holidays, and now I've been
told this is a must at every Thanksgiving dinner!*

1/4 c. plus 2 T. caramel ice
   cream topping, divided
9-inch graham cracker crust
1/2 c. plus 2 T. pecan pieces,
   divided
1 c. milk
2 3.4-oz. pkgs. instant vanilla
   pudding mix

1 c. canned pumpkin
1 t. cinnamon
1/2 t. nutmeg
8-oz. container frozen whipped
   topping, thawed and divided

Pour 1/4 cup caramel topping into crust; sprinkle with 1/2 cup nuts.
Beat milk, dry pudding mixes, pumpkin and spices with a whisk
until blended. Stir in 1-1/2 cups whipped topping; spread mixture
into crust. Refrigerate at least one hour. Before serving, spread with
remaining whipped topping, drizzle with remaining caramel topping
and sprinkle with remaining pecans. Serves 10.

Whip up this yummy dessert in only a couple of minutes!
Fold 1-1/2 cups whipped topping into a 15-3/4 ounce can
of chocolate pie filling. Spoon into dessert dishes and
garnish with chocolate cookie crumbles.

Spiced Orange Pecans

Debi DeVore
Dover, OH

A tasty hostess gift that's sure to be welcome.

2 egg whites, beaten
3 T. orange juice
2 c. pecan halves
1-1/2 c. powdered sugar
2 T. cornstarch

1 T. orange zest
1 t. cinnamon
3/4 t. ground cloves
1/4 t. allspice
1/8 t. salt

Combine egg whites and orange juice. Add pecans and toss to coat; drain. In a separate bowl, combine remaining ingredients. Add pecans and toss to coat. Spread in a single layer in a greased 15"x10" jelly-roll pan. Bake at 250 degrees for 30 to 35 minutes, or until dry and lightly golden. Cool completely; store in airtight container. Makes about 3-1/2 cups.

Before displaying gourds and pumpkins as a centerpiece, a quick wash will help them last longer. Stir together a tablespoon of bleach in a gallon of water, then gently wash and pat dry.

Marshmallow Bars

Paula Coome
Albuquerque, NM

I grew up in a Norwegian household and Scandinavian traditions were held sacred. Every Thanksgiving our family would bundle up and drive 50 miles to visit our Norwegian relatives in Watertown, South Dakota. The morning after Thanksgiving, our hosts would wake us with traditional egg coffee and these yummy marshmallow bars. This recipe has been in our family for over 30 years. Making these bars brings back many happy Thanksgiving memories. And always, thoughts of Herdis Eggen, the best hostess in town!

2 eggs, beaten
3/4 c. sugar
1/2 c. margarine
1 t. vanilla extract
2-1/2 c. graham crackers, crushed

1/2 c. chopped nuts
1/2 c. flaked coconut
2-1/2 c. mini marshmallows
11-oz. pkg. butterscotch chips
3 T. creamy peanut butter

In a saucepan over medium-high heat, combine eggs, sugar, margarine and vanilla. Cook until thick; set aside to cool. Stir in graham crackers, nuts, coconut and marshmallows. Mix together well and pat into a greased 13"x9" baking pan. In a separate saucepan over medium heat, stir together butterscotch chips and peanut butter until melted and smooth; spread over bars and set aside to cool. Cut into bars. Makes 1-1/2 dozen.

Write a sweet word of thanks or harvest quotes on strips of paper and fasten to the outside of glasses with double-sided tape. When Thanksgiving guests are seated, invite them to read the quote aloud.

Maple Syrup Cookies

Francie Stutzman
Dalton, OH

These cookies are good to serve to your kids with milk when they come home from school on a cool fall day.

1 t. baking soda
1 T. milk
1 egg, beaten
1/2 c. plus 2 T. shortening
1 c. maple syrup

3 c. all-purpose flour
1 T. baking powder
1/2 t. salt
1 t. vanilla extract
10-oz. pkg. chocolate chips

Dissolve baking soda in milk; set aside. Stir together egg, shortening and syrup until mixture is smooth. Add flour, baking powder, salt, vanilla and baking soda mixture; blend well. Stir in chocolate chips. Drop by teaspoonfuls onto greased baking sheets. Bake at 350 degrees for 12 to 14 minutes. Makes 4 dozen.

Try making camp bread for dessert…a yummy bonfire treat! Cut a loaf of unsliced bread into thick slices, then tear. Dip pieces into your favorite French toast batter and toast over the fire as you would marshmallows. Cool and dip into butter and syrup if you'd like.

Cinnamon-Glazed Apple Pie
Elizabeth Blackstone
Racine, WI

*This is one of those "must-haves" when the ladies at our church
bring dessert to the men's chili cook-off in the fall.*

9-inch pie crust
1-1/2 c. sour cream
14-oz. can sweetened
    condensed milk
1/4 c. frozen apple juice
    concentrate, thawed

1 egg, beaten
1-1/2 t. vanilla extract
1/4 t. cinnamon
3 Granny Smith apples, cored,
    peeled and thinly sliced
2 T. butter

Place crust in a pie plate and bake at 375 degrees for 15 minutes.
Blend together sour cream, sweetened condensed milk, apple juice,
egg, vanilla and cinnamon until smooth. Pour into baked pie crust.
Bake at 375 degrees for 30 minutes, or until center is set; cool. In a
skillet over medium heat, cook apples in butter until apples are
tender but still hold their shape. Arrange over pie filling; drizzle with
Cinnamon Glaze. Serve warm or chilled. Store leftovers covered in
refrigerator. Serves 8.

Cinnamon Glaze:

1/4 c. frozen apple juice
    concentrate, thawed

1 t. cornstarch
1/4 t. cinnamon

Combine ingredients in a saucepan over low heat; blend well. Cook
and stir until mixture is thickened.

Add a sprinkle of pumpkin or apple
pie spice into glasses of warm spiced
cider...so nice served with dessert.

Mother's Icebox Cookies

Linda Barker
Mount Pleasant, TN

My mother made these cookies for my sister and me when we were growing up in the 1940s and 1950s. If hickory nuts were plentiful that year, she would use them.

1/2 c. margarine
1 c. sugar
2 t. vanilla extract
1 egg, beaten
1-3/4 c. all-purpose flour

1/2 t. baking soda
1/2 t. salt
1/2 c. chopped pecans or
   English walnuts

Beat together margarine and sugar until mixture is fluffy. Add vanilla and egg, blending well. Whisk together flour, baking soda and salt; stir in nuts. Gradually add to margarine mixture; beat well. Place dough on wax paper; shape into 2 long rolls, 2 inches in diameter. Chill overnight, or, if desired, wrap and freeze for future use. Slice dough 1/4-inch thick; bake on ungreased baking sheets at 400 degrees for about 7 minutes, or until lightly golden. Makes 6 dozen.

A few days ago I walked along the edge of the lake
and was treated to the crunch and rustle of leaves
with each step I made.

~Eric Sloane

Warm & Wonderful Spice Cookies

Margie Bush
Peoria, IL

There's just something special about a kitchen when it's filled with the aromas of cinnamon, cloves and ginger.

2-1/2 c. all-purpose flour
2 t. baking soda
1/2 t. ground cloves
1/2 t. allspice
1/2 t. cinnamon
1/4 t. ground ginger

3/4 c. butter
1 c. sugar
1 egg, beaten
1/4 c. light molasses
Garnish: powdered sugar

Combine flour, baking soda and spices; set aside. In a large bowl, beat butter, sugar and egg with an electric mixer on medium speed until mixture is light and fluffy. Alternately add flour mixture and molasses to butter mixture. Cover and refrigerate dough at least one hour to overnight. When ready to bake, shape dough into 1/2-inch balls and roll in powdered sugar. Place one inch apart on greased baking sheets. Bake at 350 degrees for 8 to 10 minutes, or until lightly golden. Remove to a wire rack to cool; sprinkle with powdered sugar while still warm. Makes 4 dozen.

Pull out all your favorite fall cookie cutters and make an afternoon of Bake & Take! Invite girlfriends over to bake and decorate favorite cut-out cookies while catching up on the latest news. When it's time to say goodbye, they'll have oodles of fresh-baked cookies to take home to their families.

Quick Apple Dumplings

Ruth Miller
North Apollo, PA

Apple dumplings are a must during harvest season! If you can make a trip to the orchard, fresh-picked apples just can't be beat.

8-oz. tube refrigerated crescent
   rolls
2 Granny Smith apples, cored,
   peeled and quartered
1/8 t. cinnamon
1/2 c. butter

1 c. sugar
1 c. orange juice
1 t. vanilla extract
1/2 c. pecans, very finely
   chopped
Optional: ice cream

Unroll and separate crescent roll dough into triangles. Wrap each piece of apple in a crescent roll. Arrange in a greased 8"x8" baking pan; sprinkle with cinnamon. Combine butter, sugar and orange juice in a medium saucepan. Bring to a boil; remove from heat and stir in vanilla. Pour mixture over dumplings; sprinkle pecans over top. Bake at 350 degrees for 30 minutes, or until crust is golden and beginning to bubble. To serve, spoon some of the syrup from the baking pan over dumplings. Serve with ice cream, if desired. Serves 8.

Scoops of ice cream are perfect alongside warm apple dumplings, cobblers and pies. To make them ahead of time, simply scoop servings and arrange on a baking sheet, then pop into the freezer. When frozen, store scoops in a freezer bag, then remove as many as needed at dessert time.

Aunt Beth's Peanut Butter Chiffon Pie

Lori Rogers
Chatham, IL

This recipe was given to me by my Aunt Beth years ago. We all fell in love with the smoothness of the peanut butter chiffon filling paired with the pretzel pie crust. This is always a much-requested recipe!

1 c. pretzels, finely crushed
6 T. butter, melted
3/4 c. plus 3 T. sugar, divided
1 env. unflavored gelatin
1/4 t. salt
1 c. milk

2 eggs, separated
1/2 c. creamy peanut butter
1-1/2 c. frozen whipped
  topping, thawed
Garnish: chocolate syrup

Combine pretzel crumbs with butter and 3 tablespoons sugar. Press into an ungreased 9" pie plate and bake at 350 degrees for 8 minutes. Cool completely. Mix gelatin, 1/2 cup sugar and salt in a saucepan. Add milk and egg yolks. Cook over medium heat until boiling, stirring constantly. Remove from heat and stir in peanut butter; stir until smooth. Refrigerate until chilled. Beat egg whites with an electric mixer until foamy. Gradually stir in remaining 1/4 cup sugar and beat until stiff peaks form. Fold chilled peanut butter mixture into egg whites. When combined, gently fold in whipped topping. Spread mixture into prepared pretzel crust. Chill 2 to 3 hours, or until set. Garnish with chocolate syrup, drizzled in a criss-cross pattern. Makes 8 servings.

Clear glass votives can be made into the prettiest fall mantel lights. Cut strips of fall-colored tissue paper and arrange on the outside of votive holders with découpage medium. Seal them to the glass with another coat of découpage medium, then let dry before tucking candles inside.

Coffee Toffee

Sharon Demers
Dolores, CO

My husband loves to roast his own coffee beans and we decided to try adding them to a favorite toffee recipe. The result is delicious!

1 c. espresso beans, slightly
   crushed
1/2 c. butter

3/4 c. brown sugar, packed
1 c. semi-sweet chocolate chips

Sprinkle crushed coffee beans evenly over the bottom of an ungreased 8"x8" baking pan. Combine butter and brown sugar in a saucepan over medium-low heat; bring to a boil. Cook, stirring constantly, for exactly 7 minutes. Immediately pour mixture over crushed beans and quickly spread from side to side. Sprinkle evenly with chocolate chips. Cover pan and let sit for 5 minutes. Remove cover and spread melted chocolate chips evenly over the toffee. Refrigerate for one to 3 hours. Invert pan and break toffee into pieces. Makes about one pound.

Mason jars filled with sweet treats like candy and bite-size cookies are so nice for gift-giving. For a farmhouse touch, search out barn sales for old-fashioned jars with zinc lids.

White Chocolate Cookies

Bunny Palmertree
Carrollton, MS

This cookie recipe is the one my husband requests during the holidays. The ginger and almond extract are the ingredients that give them their special taste.

1/2 c. butter, softened
1/2 c. shortening
3/4 c. brown sugar, packed
1/2 c. sugar
1 egg, beaten
1/2 t. almond extract
2 c. all-purpose flour
1 t. baking soda

1/4 t. salt
1/4 t. cinnamon
1/4 t. ground ginger
6-oz. pkg. white baking
   chocolate, chopped
1-1/2 c. chopped pecans

Stir butter, shortening and sugars together until smooth. Add egg and extract; mix well. In a separate bowl, combine remaining ingredients except chocolate and pecans; stir into butter mixture. Blend in chocolate and pecans. Drop by rounded teaspoonfuls 2 inches apart onto greased baking sheets. Bake at 350 degrees for 8 to 10 minutes, or until lightly golden. Remove to wire racks to cool. Makes 10 dozen.

Cookies and milk just go together. Add a dash of Halloween "magic" to glasses of milk. Add a few drops of green food coloring to the milk carton and gently shake. Just watch their faces as you pour the milk!

Mixed-Up Cupcakes

Janie Saey
Wentzville, MO

*My girlfriend gave me this yummy recipe in 1974. And yes,
you really do frost them before baking!*

1/3 c. shortening	2 t. baking powder
1 c. sugar	1/2 t. salt
2 eggs, separated	1/2 c. light brown sugar,
1/2 c. milk	packed
1 t. vanilla extract	2 T. baking cocoa
1-2/3 c. all-purpose flour	1/4 c. chopped pecans

Combine shortening and sugar; blend until smooth. Add one egg plus one yolk, milk and vanilla. Sift together flour, baking powder and salt; stir into shortening mixture until smooth. Fill paper-lined muffin cups 1/2 full; set aside. Beat remaining egg white with an electric mixer at high speed until stiff peaks form. Add brown sugar and cocoa; beat until well blended. Spoon a generous teaspoonful over each cupcake; sprinkle with nuts. Bake at 350 for 20 minutes. Makes 12 to 15.

Protect your table from hot dishes with autumn leaf trivets. They're easily made from wool felt. Simply cut out oversize leaves in any shape you like (you can use a disappearing-ink fabric pen to make a pattern before cutting). When ready to use, simply layer them down the center of the table where hot dishes will be placed.

Spicy Applesauce Pie

Carol Hickman
Kingsport, TN

I tweaked my original recipe by adding a crumb topping to it, and I've decided I like it better this way! I recommend the chunky applesauce variety, or use the cinnamon variety if you want to give the pie even more flavor.

1/4 c. butter, softened
1/2 c. sugar or 2/3 c.
   unsweetened applesauce
2 eggs, beaten
2 c. sweetened applesauce

1/2 t. vanilla extract
1/4 to 1/2 t. cinnamon
Optional: 1/4 t. ground cloves,
   1/4 t. nutmeg
9-inch pie crust

Combine butter, sugar and eggs; beat until smooth. Add applesauce, vanilla and spices and mix thoroughly. Pour mixture into pie crust. Sprinkle with Crumb Topping. Bake at 425 degrees for 35 to 45 minutes, or until center is set. Serves 8.

Crumb Topping:

1 c. all-purpose flour
1/2 c. light brown sugar,
   packed
1/2 t. cinnamon

1/2 c. chilled butter, diced
1/2 c. quick-cooking oats,
   uncooked

In a food processor or blender, combine flour, sugar and cinnamon. Add butter and pulse until large crumbs form. Add oats and pulse mixture just until combined.

Scrumptious slices of pie can double as yummy guest favors. Package them in pretty parchment paper-lined boxes and tie on a tag.

Grandma Ila's Pumpkin Cookies

Kristin Pittis
Dennison, OH

This is an old family recipe passed down from Grandma.

1 c. shortening
1 c. sugar
1 c. canned pumpkin
1 egg, beaten
2 t. vanilla extract, divided
2 c. all-purpose flour
1/2 t. salt

1 t. baking soda
1 t. baking powder
1 t. cinnamon
8-oz. pkg. cream cheese,
  softened
1/4 c. butter, softened
2 c. powdered sugar

Blend together shortening, sugar, pumpkin and egg; stir in one teaspoon vanilla. Combine remaining ingredients except cream cheese, butter and powdered sugar. Gradually beat flour mixture into pumpkin mixture. Drop by rounded tablespoonfuls onto greased baking sheets. Bake at 350 degrees for 12 to 15 minutes; cool completely. Blend together cream cheese and butter; stir in remaining vanilla. Gradually add powdered sugar until fluffy. Spread cookies with frosting. Makes 2 to 3 dozen.

Whisk a cup of heavy cream until soft peaks form,
then gently whisk in a tablespoon of maple syrup...
heavenly served over slices of warm pie!

Favorite Zucchini Brownies

Jennifer Tanner
Smethport, PA

*This is a wonderful way to eat zucchini! If you'd like,
double the recipe and bake in a 13"x9" baking pan.*

1/4 c. butter, melted
1 c. sugar
1 egg, beaten
1 t. vanilla extract
1 c. all-purpose flour
1 t. baking powder
1/2 t. baking soda
1 T. water

1/2 t. salt
2-1/2 T. baking cocoa
1/2 c. chopped walnuts
3/4 c. zucchini, shredded
1/2 c. semi-sweet
   chocolate chips

Add butter to a large bowl; blend in remaining ingredients except
chocolate chips. Blend well. Spread into a greased 8"x8" baking pan;
sprinkle batter with chocolate chips. Bake at 350 degrees for
35 minutes. Cool before cutting. Makes one dozen.

When the zucchini harvest is at its peak, freeze extras for
use all winter long for your favorite sweet recipes like
breads and brownies. Shred as much zucchini
as the recipe calls for, then steam it for one to
2 minutes. Cool and pack pre-measured
amounts into containers, leaving 1/2-inch
headspace. Seal, label and freeze. When
using in a recipe, thaw and add to
ingredients, reducing the amount
of liquid if needed.

FALL FESTIVAL

Favorites

Barbecue Chicken Wings

Beth Bundy
Long Prairie, MN

Partially baked, partially cooked in the slow cooker, these wings have a zippy flavor...they get even better the longer they cook!

3 lbs. chicken wings
2 c. catsup
1/2 c. honey
2 T. lemon juice
2 T. oil
1 T. paprika

4 cloves garlic, minced
1 t. curry powder
1/2 t. salt
1/2 t. pepper
1/8 t. hot pepper sauce

Arrange wings on a greased baking sheet. Whisk remaining ingredients together and pour over wings. Bake, uncovered, at 350 degrees for 40 minutes, or until juices run clear. After baking, place in a slow cooker, cover and cook on low setting 2 to 3 hours. Serves 12.

When it comes to tailgating dippers, serve up lots of variety. Hearty crackers, pretzel rods, crisp veggies or slices of thick sourdough or pumpernickel bread. All are just right for creamy dips and spreads.

Fall Festival Favorites

Blue Cheese Spread

Marion Sundberg
Ramona, CA

While on vacation, we stopped at a wonderful California winery to taste wine. They had something similar to this yummy spread to eat while tasting their sparkling wine.

8-oz. pkg. cream cheese,
  softened
4-oz. pkg. crumbled blue cheese
1/4 to 1/2 c. dry sparkling
  white wine or sparkling
  white grape juice

cracked pepper to taste
1/2 c. chopped pecans
1/4 c. fresh chives, snipped
assorted crackers

Combine cream cheese and blue cheese. Stir in wine, champagne or grape juice until desired consistency is reached. Add remaining ingredients except crackers; blend well. Serve with crackers. Serves 12.

Crabmeat Dip

Danyel Martin
Madisonville, KY

This recipe was given to me by my mom. It is wonderful to take to a potluck for work or a family gathering. I took this to a black-tie event with my husband's boss and it was the hit of the party.

8-oz. pkg. cream cheese,
  softened
1 t. lemon juice
2 t. onion, minced

1-1/2 T. crumbled blue cheese
12-oz. jar cocktail sauce
6-oz. can crabmeat, drained
club crackers

Blend together cream cheese, lemon juice, minced onion and blue cheese. Spread evenly on a plate; spread with cocktail sauce to cover. Sprinkle with crabmeat. Serve with crackers. Serves 20.

Pineapple-Pecan Cheese Spread

Cynde Sonnier
Mont Belvieu, TX

This is a delicious fast-fix recipe and yummy with fresh veggies.

2 8-oz. pkgs. cream cheese, softened
1-1/2 c. shredded Cheddar cheese
1 c. chopped pecans, toasted and divided
3/4 c. crushed pineapple, drained

4-oz. can chopped green chiles, drained
2 T. roasted red peppers, chopped
1/2 t. garlic powder

In a large bowl, beat cream cheese until smooth. Add Cheddar cheese, 3/4 cup pecans, pineapple, chiles, red pepper and garlic powder; beat until thoroughly combined. Transfer to a serving dish. Cover and refrigerate. When ready to serve, sprinkle with remaining pecans. Serves 8.

Keep an eye out at flea markets for woolly blankets. They make perfect tailgating tablecloths, and will keep you toasty warm during a chilly Friday night game!

Cheddar Apple Pie Dip

Cindy Snyder
Kittanning, PA

This is a great appetizer for a fall gathering of friends around a toasty fire.

1/4 c. brown sugar, packed
1/4 t. cinnamon
1 red apple, cored and finely chopped
1 Granny Smith apple, cored and finely chopped
1/2 c. pecan pieces, coarsely chopped

8-oz. pkg. cream cheese, softened
1-1/2 c. shredded sharp Cheddar cheese
1/2 c. sour cream

Combine brown sugar and cinnamon in a bowl; stir in apples and pecans. Mix cream cheese and Cheddar cheese; add sour cream, stirring well to blend. Spread mixture in a 9" pie plate; top with apple mixture. Bake, uncovered, at 375 degrees for 20 minutes, or until heated through. Serves 6 to 8.

Give bottles of cream soda, root beer or lemonade a bit of hometown pride for a pre-game party. Choose papers in school colors to wrap around each bottle, then top off with a tag and mini pompom.

Slow-Cooker Roast Beef Sandwiches

Deborah Griggs
Lexington, TN

This is delicious and can be served with your favorite chips or French fries. Try spooning it on mini buns for easy-to-hold sandwiches.

1.05-oz. env. Italian salad
   dressing mix
1-oz. env. au jus gravy mix
2 c. hot water
2 T. Worcestershire sauce

2 to 3-lb. beef rump roast
8 to 12 buns, split and toasted
8-oz. pkg. mozzarella cheese
   slices

Whisk dry mixes in hot water; stir in Worcestershire sauce until mixture is smooth. Arrange roast in a slow cooker; pour mixture over the roast. Cover and cook on low setting for 10 to 12 hours. Transfer roast to a platter and shred with 2 forks. Spoon onto buns; top with cheese. If desired, serve remaining juices from slow cooker as dipping sauce for sandwiches. Makes 8 to 12 servings.

A vintage metal cooler is as good as ever for keeping soda, cider and juice frosty for family get-togethers or neighborhood block parties.

Fall Festival *Favorites*

Chili-Cornbread Salad

Rachel Keim
Millersburg, OH

I've been making this recipe for 5 years. I get so many requests for it, and I've never heard anyone say they don't like it. I also like to use my own frozen corn and shred cheese myself for more flavor.

8-1/2 oz. pkg. cornbread
   muffin mix
4-oz. can chopped green chiles
1/8 t. ground cumin
1/8 t. dried oregano
1/8 t. dried sage
1 c. mayonnaise
1 c. sour cream
1-oz. env. ranch salad
   dressing mix

2 15-oz. cans pinto beans,
   drained and rinsed
2 15-1/2 oz. cans corn,
   drained
3 tomatoes, chopped
1 c. green pepper, chopped
1 c. onion, chopped
10 slices bacon, crisply cooked
   and crumbled
2 c. shredded Cheddar cheese

Prepare cornbread batter according to package directions; stir in chiles and seasonings. Spread in a greased 8"x8" baking pan. Bake at 400 degrees for 20 to 25 minutes, or until center tests done; set aside to cool. In a small bowl, combine mayonnaise, sour cream and ranch dressing mix; set aside. Crumble half of the cornbread into a lightly greased 13"x9" baking pan. Layer with half each of beans, mayonnaise mixture, corn, tomatoes, green pepper, onion, bacon and cheese. Repeat layers. Cover and refrigerate for 2 hours. Serves 12.

Keep all your favorite fall recipes right at your fingertips. Keep recipe cards organized in a retro tin lunchbox...how fun!

Fast & Easy Red Pepper Hummus

Kathy Harris
Valley Center, KS

I experimented with several recipes and came up with this quick, easy and delicious new one. Our friends just love it served with pita chips.

2 15-oz. cans chickpeas,
  drained and rinsed
2 T. taco seasoning mix

1 c. roasted red peppers,
  chopped
olive oil to taste

Purèe chickpeas, taco seasoning and roasted red peppers together in a food processor. Drizzle in olive oil until desired consistency is reached. Chill one hour before serving. Makes 2 cups.

Homebaked Pita Chips

Nola Coons
Gooseberry Patch

These crispy, crunchy chips are ready in no time at all!

6 pita rounds, halved and split   1 T. kosher salt

Cut each pita half into 8 to 12 wedges. Arrange on an aluminum-foil lined baking sheet. Spray chips with non-stick vegetable spray; sprinkle with salt. Broil for 3 to 5 minutes, until golden. Serves 6 to 10.

Delicious autumn! My very soul is wedded to it,
and if I were a bird I would fly about the earth
seeking the successive autumns.

~George Eliot

Cincinnati-Style Chili Dip

Tara Horton
Gooseberry Patch

*It's just not a tailgate party in Cincinnati unless this warm dip
is passed around. Try to find a chili with cinnamon
for an authentic Queen City experience!*

8-oz. pkg. cream cheese,
  softened
10-1/2 oz. can chili without
  beans

8-oz. pkg. shredded mild
  Cheddar cheese
tortilla chips

Spread cream cheese in an ungreased 8"x8" baking pan. Pour chili
over top and sprinkle with cheese. Bake, uncovered, at 350 degrees
for 10 to 15 minutes, until cheese is melted. Serve with tortilla
chips. Serves 10.

Buffalo Wing Dip

Amanda Coomer
Franklin, OH

*Every time I take this somewhere I come home with an empty pan.
Everyone loves it and I always get many requests for the recipe.*

2 8-oz. pkgs. cream cheese,
  softened
15-oz. jar chunky blue cheese
  salad dressing
2 boneless, skinless chicken
  breasts, cooked and
  shredded

12-oz. bottle chicken
  wing sauce
8-oz. pkg. shredded Monterey
  Jack and Cheddar cheese
  blend
tortilla chips or crackers

Blend together cream cheese and salad dressing until smooth.
Spread in the bottom of an ungreased 8"x8" baking pan. Combine
chicken and sauce together; spoon over cream cheese mixture.
Sprinkle shredded cheese on top. Bake, uncovered, at 350 degrees
until cheese is melted and dip is heated through. Serve with tortilla
chips or crackers. Serves 10.

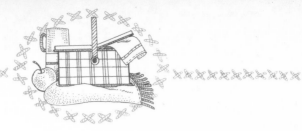

Peanut Butter Bars

Theresa Wehmeyer
Rosebud, MO

This recipe is loved by both my kids!

1/2 c. margarine, softened
1/2 c. sugar
1/2 c. brown sugar, packed
1/2 c. plus 2 T. creamy peanut
   butter, divided
1 egg, beaten
1 t. vanilla extract
1 c. all-purpose flour

1/2 c. quick-cooking oats,
   uncooked
1 t. baking soda
1/4 t. salt
1 c. semi-sweet chocolate chips
1/2 c. powdered sugar
2 T. milk

Combine margarine, sugars and 1/2 cup peanut butter until smooth. Add egg and vanilla; mix well. Combine flour, oats, baking soda and salt; stir into margarine mixture. Spread into a greased 13"x9" baking pan; sprinkle with chocolate chips. Bake at 350 degrees for 20 to 25 minutes, or until lightly golden; set aside to cool 10 minutes. Combine powdered sugar, milk and remaining peanut butter until smooth; drizzle over bars. Cut into bars. Makes 16 to 18 bars.

Enjoy football fever even if you don't have tickets to the big game. Invite friends and neighbors over to watch the game on TV...you can enjoy all your favorite foods while cheering on your team!

Raspberry Crumb Cookie Bars

Andrea Heyart
Aubrey, TX

This recipe has become an often-requested dessert at family gatherings and holiday parties.

1 c. sugar
1 c. plus 1 T. all-purpose flour, divided
1/4 c. butter, diced
18-oz. tube refrigerated sugar cookie dough, softened

8-oz. pkg. cream cheese, softened
12-oz. jar seedless raspberry jam

Whisk together sugar and one cup flour. Stir in butter with a fork until mixture resembles coarse crumbs. Set aside. Blend cookie dough and cream cheese with an electric mixer on medium speed until smooth. Add remaining flour if mixture is too soft. Press into the bottom of a greased 13"x9" baking pan. Bake at 350 degrees for 8 minutes. Let cool slightly, then spread jam over crust. Sprinkle sugar mixture over jam; return to oven for an additional 10 minutes. Let cool and cut into bars. Refrigerate any leftovers. Makes one dozen bars.

Whether you're bringing drop or cut-out cookies, brownies or bars, wrap each individually in wax-paper bags and tuck them in a picnic basket for easy toting. They'll arrive tasting oven-fresh and the bags will keep crisp cookies from drying out softer ones.

Raspberry Chipotle Dip

Linda Vogt
Las Vegas, NV

I have made this for the past couple of years and it is delish! You can't stop eating it once you start!

2 8-oz. pkgs. cream cheese, softened
15-oz. bottle roasted raspberry chipotle sauce, divided

assorted crackers

Arrange blocks of cream cheese side-by-side on a serving plate. Pour one cup raspberry chipotle sauce over cream cheese, reserving remaining sauce for another recipe. Serve with assorted crackers. Serves 20.

Cashew-Chili Cheese Ball

Paula Marchesi
Lenhartsville, PA

This cheese ball was my favorite every time my mom made it...my brother and I couldn't wait until it was ready! Now I serve it at all my family gatherings. Often I'll swap out the chili powder and substitute cayenne pepper, black pepper, cumin or curry powder.

16-oz. pkg. pasteurized process cheese spread, softened
4-oz. pkg. cream cheese, softened
2/3 c. chopped cashews

1/2 t. garlic salt
Garnish: chili powder
assorted crackers and cocktail breads

Combine cheeses, cashews and garlic salt; cover and refrigerate 20 minutes. Shape into a ball and coat completely with chili powder. Serve with crackers and bread. Makes 3 cups.

Old-Fashioned Ginger Beer

Amy Butcher
Columbus, GA

Our family always makes homemade root beer for family gatherings, but one year we tried this recipe. From then on, it's been a must-have right alongside our root beer.

4 lemons
1 orange
3/4 c. fresh ginger, peeled and
  coarsely chopped
3/4 c. honey
3/4 c. sugar

2 c. boiling water
1-1/4 c. orange juice
4 c. sparkling mineral water,
  chilled
crushed ice

Grate 2 tablespoons of zest from lemons and orange. Set orange and one lemon aside. Squeeze 1/3 cup lemon juice from remaining 3 lemons. Set aside. In a food processor, pulse ginger, honey and sugar until just combined. Add orange and lemon zests and boiling water; stir until sugar dissolves. Cool to room temperature. Cover and refrigerate for at least 24 hours and up to 5 days. To serve, strain ginger beer base into a pitcher. Thinly slice remaining lemon and orange; add to pitcher. Stir in sparkling water. Serve over ice. Makes 8 to 10 servings.

Try making homemade root beer at home, it's so easy and so yummy! Add 5 gallons of cool water and a 4-pound bag of sugar to a large beverage cooler; stir to dissolve sugar. Blend in a 2-ounce bottle of root beer concentrate. Wearing gloves, slowly add 5 pounds of dry ice to the mixture; cover loosely with lid to allow mixture to bubble. When bubbling is complete, your root beer is ready to enjoy!

Barbecue Chicken Sandwiches

Lori Rosenberg
University Heights, OH

This is a wonderful alternative to the traditional pulled pork.

1 lb. boneless, skinless chicken
  breasts
1 onion, sliced
1 to 2 T. oil
1/2 c. barbecue sauce

1/4 c. water
1 T. brown sugar, packed
4 mini loaves ciabatta bread,
  halved lengthwise
sliced cheese of your choice

Sauté chicken and onion in oil in skillet over medium-high heat for 7 to 9 minutes, stirring occasionally. Stir in barbecue sauce, water and sugar; stir to blend. Reduce heat to medium; cover. Cook an additional 7 minutes, or until chicken is cooked through. Remove chicken from skillet. Shred chicken with a fork or chop into small pieces. Return to skillet; stir until evenly coated with sauce. Spoon chicken onto bread and add cheese slices. Serves 4.

Offer a variety of breads, rolls, buns, pita pockets and mini buns when serving sandwiches. Keep them soft and fresh by arranging in a market basket, then covering with tea towels in school colors!

Guacamole Tossed Salad

Gennell Williams
Fieldale, VA

This is the ideal salad, no matter the reason for your get-together!

2 tomatoes, chopped
1/2 red onion, sliced and
   separated into rings
6 slices bacon, crisply cooked
   and crumbled
1/3 c. oil
2 T. cider vinegar

1 t. salt
1/4 t. pepper
1/4 t. hot pepper sauce
2 avocados, pitted, peeled
   and cubed
4 c. salad greens, torn

In a bowl, combine tomatoes, onion and bacon. In a separate bowl, whisk together oil, vinegar, salt, pepper and hot pepper sauce. Pour over tomato mixture; toss gently. Add avocados. Place greens in a large serving bowl; add avocado mixture and toss to coat. Serve immediately. Makes 4 servings.

Indian summer days can be warm, even though it's fall. When heading to a tailgating get-together, keep traveling salads crisp by packing them in an ice-filled cooler. When they're ready to serve, scoop some of the cooler ice into a bowl and set the salad bowls right on top...nestle them into the ice a bit to keep them cool.

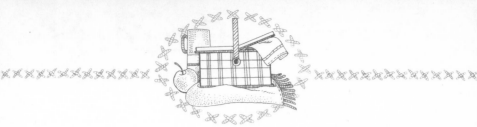

Ranch Tortilla Roll-Ups

Jamie Rodolph
Lolo, MT

Really yummy appetizers and a snap to prepare.

8-oz. pkg. cream cheese,
  softened
1-oz. env. ranch dressing mix
4 10 or 12-inch flour tortillas
2 tomatoes, chopped

2-1/4 oz. can sliced black
  olives, drained and chopped
2 T. bacon bits
1 c. shredded Cheddar cheese

Mix cream cheese and ranch dressing mix together until smooth; spread on one side of each tortilla. Sprinkle tomatoes, olives, bacon and shredded cheese evenly on top of the cream cheese mixture. Roll up tortillas and wrap each in plastic wrap; chill for one hour. When ready to serve, cut each roll into one-inch slices. Serves 10 to 12.

Marianne's Cranberry Roll-Ups

Sandi Giverson
Vero Beach, FL

One of the girls I work with, Marianne Hudgins, always has the best recipes! With her permission, here is one of my favorites.

8-oz. container whipped cream
  cheese
8-oz. pkg. crumbled feta cheese
6-oz. pkg. sweetened dried
  cranberries

4 to 5 green onions, sliced
4 10-inch flour tortillas

Combine all ingredients except tortillas together; blend until smooth. Spread mixture over tortillas, roll up and wrap in plastic wrap; chill until ready to serve. Cut each roll into one-inch slices. Serves 10.

CAMPFIRE Classics

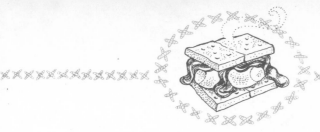

Camper's Sausage Dinner

Judi Towner
Clarks Summit, PA

My granddaughters love to help put this foil packet together for grilling. This meal is fun, easy to make and there are never any leftovers! It's a great camping recipe.

3/4 lb. green beans, trimmed and halved
1/2 lb. red potatoes, quartered
1 green or red pepper, sliced
1 onion, sliced
1 lb. smoked pork sausage or Kielbasa sausage, cut into 1-inch pieces

1 t. salt
1 t. pepper
1 t. oil
1 t. butter
1/3 c. water

On a large sheet of aluminum foil, arrange green beans, potatoes, green or red pepper, onion and sausage; season with salt and pepper. Drizzle with oil and top with butter. Fold and seal edges of foil around mixture to create a packet, leaving only a small opening in the center. Pour water into the opening; seal. Place foil packet on a campfire grate or outdoor grill over high heat. Cook 20 to 30 minutes, turning once, until sausage is browned and vegetables are tender. Serves 4 to 6.

Here are some quick tips for getting a campfire started and ready for cooking. Crumple newspaper for the first layer, then add dry twigs and leaves. Light the paper, add wood and let it burn until you get red glowing coals. Let it burn down a bit more, then place the cooking grate over the coals.

Campfire Classics

Veggie-Stuffed Tortillas

Angie Venable
Gooseberry Patch

We always make these during the fall when the kids' friends come over for a weekend bonfire. They're super-simple and everyone can make their own with favorite veggies and cheeses.

1-1/3 c. zucchini, shredded
1 c. tomato, chopped

1/2 c. crumbled feta cheese
4 8-inch flour tortillas

Place 1/3 cup zucchini, 1/4 cup tomato and 2 tablespoons cheese down the center of each tortilla. Fold to cover filling and place in a greased pie iron. Place pie iron over hot fire until tortilla is crispy and filling is heated through, 5 to 7 minutes. Repeat with remaining tortillas. Makes 4 servings.

Pie-Iron Pizza Pie

Tina Dillon
Parma, OH

Mix this recipe up as you like...make it all veggie, add pineapple and ham or swap out pepperoni for browned sausage. You can't go wrong!

8 slices white bread
margarine
1/4 c. pizza sauce

4 slices mozzarella cheese
16 slices pepperoni

Spread margarine on one side of each bread slice. Place one slice, margarine-side down, in a pie iron. Top bread with 2 tablespoons sauce, one slice cheese and 4 slices pepperoni. Top fillings with a bread slice, margarine-side up. Close pie iron and toast over hot coals for about 5 minutes. Makes 4 servings.

Chicken-Portabella Packets

Donna Bodine
Cleveland, TX

Toss these on the grill when a rainy day means no campfire. You can even bake them in a 350-degree oven for 30 to 35 minutes.

2 boneless, skinless chicken
   breast strips
1 T. Cajun seasoning
1 t. seasoning salt
2 T. olive oil, divided

2 portabella mushrooms, sliced
1/4 T. dried oregano
1/8 t. salt
1/8 t. pepper

Place chicken in a square of aluminum foil; rub with Cajun seasoning and seasoning salt. Drizzle with one tablespoon oil. Toss mushrooms with remaining oil; stir in seasonings. Spoon mushrooms over chicken; fold and seal edges of foil around mixture to create a packet. Place packet on a campfire grate or outdoor grill and cook over medium heat for 20 minutes. Serves 2.

Harvest nights are brisk, which means sitting around the fire is oh-so cozy. And you can cook the same family-favorite recipes over a campfire that you can cook on a gas or charcoal grill...hot dogs, steaks, hamburgers, chicken, even shish-kabobs!

Campfire Classics

Campfire Veggie Pack

Jaci Myers
Lafayette, IN

Our favorite way to enjoy fresh veggies. Also try zucchini or asparagus...yum! This recipe serves 4 but can easily be adjusted to serve less or even a crowd.

1 onion, thinly sliced
4 potatoes, thinly sliced
1 c. carrot, peeled and thinly
   sliced
1 c. green beans, trimmed

1 T. butter
1/8 t. dill weed or favorite
   dried herb
Optional: 1 clove garlic,
   chopped

In the center of a large sheet of heavy-duty aluminum foil, layer all ingredients in order given. Fold and seal edges of foil around mixture to create a packet. Place packet on a campfire grate or outdoor grill. Cook over medium heat for approximately 25 to 30 minutes. Serves 4.

It's a snap to clean the grate after cooking!
A little water and a scouring pad or grill brush
will do the trick. Rinse the grate well
and dry before storing.

Pie-Iron Tasty Tacos

Jason Keller
Carrollton, GA

Our kids love tacos, so we created this recipe for dinners around the campfire. What a hit!

1 lb. ground beef
1-oz. pkg. taco seasoning mix
12 5-inch corn tortillas
1 c. shredded Monterey Jack
   cheese

1/2 c. onion, chopped
Garnish: shredded lettuce,
   diced tomato, salsa and
   sour cream

Cook ground beef in a large skillet over medium-high heat until browned. Drain; stir in taco seasoning according to package directions. Spray the inside of a pie iron with non-stick vegetable spray; place a corn tortilla on one side. Add about 1/4 cup of seasoned beef on top of tortilla; sprinkle with cheese and onion. Arrange a second tortilla over filling; close pie iron. Cook over medium-hot coals until tortilla is crispy and filling is heated through, about 10 minutes. Remove from pie iron; garnish as desired. Repeat with remaining ingredients. Makes 6 servings.

Before using your pie iron for the first time, clean it with hot water, then wipe dry. Season it by giving the inside a coating of non-stick vegetable spray. Heat the pie iron over a fire for as long as you wish; let cool, then wash with plain water and coat again before storing.

Bacon-Wrapped Corn

Donna Tennant
Jasper, IN

Great to prepare ahead of time and take to a friend's cookout.

1/2 c. mayonnaise-type salad
 dressing
2 T. ranch salad dressing mix

4 ears corn, husked
4 slices bacon

Combine salad dressing and dry mix; spread over each ear of corn.
Wrap a slice of bacon around each ear of corn; lay on a sheet of
aluminum foil and wrap the corn in foil. Arrange on a campfire
grate or outdoor grill and cook over medium-high heat for
5 minutes. Turn foil packets over and grill until corn is tender,
about 10 to 15 minutes. Makes 4 servings.

Fall nights can be chilly, so whip up a no-stitch lap blanket
to keep warm in. All you need is a yard of fleece and a pair
of scissors to cut a fringe around the edges. How easy!

Chicken-Jalapeño Wraps

Cheryl Maynard
Dickinson, TX

My husband and I tried these out at our house one day, and we loved them. They're perfect for parties or just munching.

2 to 3 jalapeños, seeded, rinsed and thinly sliced
1 lb. chicken tenders, cut into bite-size pieces
8-oz. pkg. sliced Cheddar cheese, cut into cubes
1-lb. pkg. sliced bacon
Optional: barbecue sauce

Place one slice of jalapeño on each chicken tender; top with one cube of cheese. Cut bacon into sections long enough to wrap around chicken; secure with a toothpick. Arrange on an aluminum foil-lined campfire grate over hot coals, or on an outdoor grill on high heat. Cook approximately 20 minutes, or until bacon is crisp and chicken is cooked through. Makes about 30.

Make a backyard campout fun…pack the fixin's for s'mores in a hobo bag! Arrange marshmallows, chocolate bars and graham crackers in the center of a bandanna, tie the 4 corners around a stick and you're ready to go!

Pie-Iron Beef & Swiss Sandwiches
Kelly Lucyszyn
Rochester, NY

A family favorite! We know once the tent is set up, we'll be ready to put together this wonderful meal. Omit the chiles, mayo and mustard and substitute corned beef, a bit of sauerkraut and a garnish of Thousand Island dressing for a yummy Reuben sandwich.

4-oz. can green chiles, chopped
2 T. mayonnaise
1 T. Dijon mustard
2 T. butter, softened

10 slices rye bread
5 slices Swiss cheese
10 slices deli roast beef
Garnish: salsa or picante sauce

Blend together chiles, mayonnaise and mustard; set aside. Spread butter on one side of each bread slice; arrange bread, butter-side down, in one side of a pie iron. Spread one tablespoon chile mixture on each unbuttered side of bread. Layer each sandwich with one slice of cheese, 2 slices of beef and remaining bread slice. Close pie iron and cook over hot coals until golden, about 7 minutes. Serves 5.

Your pie iron will come apart at the hinges...this creates 2 mini frying pans. Just right for frying eggs at breakfast!

Pineapple-Mallow Pies

Shelley Turner
Boise, ID

A sweet treat we enjoy as we settle in to sleep under the stars.

2 T. butter, softened
8 slices bread
15-1/4 oz. can crushed
  pineapple, drained

1 to 1-1/4 c. mini
  marshmallows

Spread butter over 2 slices of bread. Place first slice, butter-side down, in one side of a pie iron. Top bread with about 1/4 cup pineapple; sprinkle generously with marshmallows. Place second slice of bread over marshmallows, buttered-side up; close pie iron. Toast over medium-hot coals until marshmallows are melted and pies are golden, about 10 minutes. Repeat to make 3 more pies. Serves 4.

Fireside Banana Splits

Sarah Oravecz
Gooseberry Patch

You can't go wrong with this recipe...it's always a hit!

6 bananas, unpeeled with
  stems removed
12-oz. pkg. semi-sweet
  chocolate chips

10-1/2 oz. pkg. mini
  marshmallows

Lightly spray 4 sheets of aluminum foil with non-stick vegetable spray. Slice each banana peel lengthwise, while also slicing the banana inside. Carefully open banana wide enough to sprinkle desired amount of chocolate chips and marshmallows inside. Wrap filled bananas in aluminum foil. Place on an outdoor grill over high heat, or directly in the coals of a campfire. Leave over heat long enough to melt chips and marshmallows, about 5 minutes. To serve, carefully unwrap foil and pull peels apart. Makes 6 servings.

Campfire Classics

Grilled Peaches & Pineapple

Judith Zechman
Butler, PA

A yummy ending to any outdoor meal.

1/2 c. orange juice
1/4 c. vinegar
1/4 c. oil
1/4 c. soy sauce
1/2 t. salt

1/8 t. nutmeg
15-oz. can sliced peaches,
  drained
20-oz. can pineapple chunks,
  drained

Whisk together all ingredients except fruit; pour into a plastic zipping bag. Add fruit to bag and marinate one hour. Discard marinade. Place fruit in the center of a large sheet of heavy-duty aluminum foil. Fold and seal edges of foil around fruit to create a packet. Place on a campfire grate or outdoor grill and cook over medium heat for 8 to 10 minutes. Serves 4.

Sweet Potato Foil Packs

Lori Cagle
Maggie Valley, NC

One of our favorite Girl Scout campfire meals!

4 sweet potatoes, peeled and
  thinly sliced
6 T. butter, sliced

1/4 c. brown sugar, packed
1 c. mini marshmallows

Arrange potatoes in a single layer on a sheet of heavy-duty aluminum foil; top with butter slices. Sprinkle with brown sugar and marshmallows; fold and seal edges of foil around mixture to create a packet. Place packets on a second sheet of foil and wrap again. Arrange on hot coals; cook for 20 minutes, turning every 5 minutes. Serves 4.

Mom's Muffin Cup Breakfast

Wendy Jacobs
Idaho Falls, ID

I always make this for breakfast when we're camping, even if it's only a sleepover in the backyard. It's super-easy to make and everyone loves it.

6 eggs
3/4 c. cooked ham, chopped
3/4 c. shredded Cheddar cheese

1-1/2 c. potatoes, peeled
   and diced
salt and pepper to taste

Coat the insides of 6 muffin cups with non-stick vegetable spray. Break one egg into each muffin cup; sprinkle with cheese and ham. To remaining 6 cups, add potatoes; season with salt and pepper. Place muffin tin on a campfire grate. Cook over hot coals for 20 minutes, or until eggs are set. Serves 6.

Pie-Iron Breakfast Burritos

Samantha Stanko
Dayton, OH

Simple to make and really filling.

4 8-inch flour tortillas
4 eggs, scrambled
1 c. shredded cheddar cheese

1 green pepper, chopped
1 onion, chopped
Garnish: salsa

Fill each tortilla with 1/4 of the scrambled eggs; top with cheese, pepper and onion. Fold over sides and ends of tortillas; arrange each in a greased pie iron. Cook over hot coals for 5 minutes. Serves 4.

Pie irons can be found in all shapes...round, square and even ones made just to fit hot dogs!

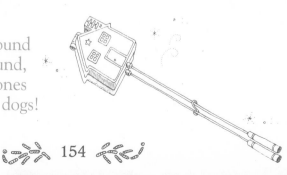

Grilled Potatoes with Herbs

Jami Rodolph
Lolo, MT

*These are really yummy with ranch dressing or fresh
lemon juice drizzled on top right before serving.*

1 lb. redskin or gold potatoes,
  peeled and chopped
2 t. garlic, chopped
1 T. fresh parsley, chopped
1 T. fresh basil, chopped

2 to 3 t. kosher salt
1 t. pepper
2 T. olive oil
2 T. butter, sliced

Arrange potatoes on a large sheet of heavy-duty aluminum foil.
Sprinkle with garlic, parsley, basil, salt and pepper; drizzle with oil.
Toss lightly to coat potatoes; dot with butter. Wrap aluminum foil
around the potatoes and seal ends. Place packet on a campfire grate
or outdoor grill over medium heat for 30 to 45 minutes. Serves 4.

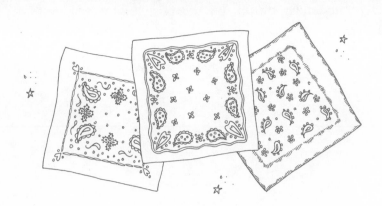

Remember making a comfy sit-upon as a kid?
They're so easy to whip up and perfect for camping or
sitting around the backyard fire pit. Lay 2 bandannas
on top of each other; stitch around 3 sides. Slip fiberfill
into the opening to make it nice and comfy, then
slip-stitch the opening closed.

Rebecca's Campfire Packets

*Rebecca Reynoso
Okeechobee, FL*

Very delicious and a breeze to whip up!

4 to 6 red potatoes, thinly sliced
1 red, green, yellow or orange
  pepper, cut into 1/4-inch
  strips
1 onion, sliced
2 T. olive oil

2 T. steak seasoning salt
Optional: 1 T. garlic, minced
salt and pepper to taste
4 precooked chicken sausages,
  thinly sliced

Divide potatoes evenly among 4 sheets of aluminum foil that have
been lightly coated with non-stick vegetable spray. Top potatoes
with pepper and onion; drizzle with oil. Sprinkle with seasoning salt,
garlic, salt and pepper, if desired. Arrange sausage slices on top.
Wrap foil securely to form a packet; place on a campfire grate or
outdoor grill over medium heat. Cook 14 to 18 minutes, or until
potatoes are tender, turning packets once during cooking time.
Serves 4.

Once the sun goes down, have some good old-fashioned
fun making shadow puppets, catching a jar of fireflies,
playing flashlight tag and telling ghost stories. It's all
about making memories that will last.

Campfire Classics

Mom's Best Marinade

Lorna Petersen
Burbank, WA

When we went camping, we always marinated our steak or chicken with this recipe. So easy to follow, just place the meat in a bowl, pierce it slightly with a fork, then top with the marinade. Marinate meat in the refrigerator for 2 hours to 2 days and grill using your favorite recipe.

1/2 c. soy sauce
1/8 t. garlic, minced
2 T. brown sugar, packed

1 t. ground ginger
2 T. vinegar

Mix all ingredients together. Makes about 3/4 cup.

Pork Chop Rub

Amy Allen
Monticello, IN

This recipe has been with our family since my husband and I were married 10 years ago. It's so easy to use…simply rub on both sides of your pork chops, set aside for 15 to 30 minutes, then grill to desired doneness.

1 T. brown sugar, packed
1-1/2 t. chili powder
1/4 t. salt

1/4 t. pepper
1/4 t. ground cumin
1/8 t. allspice

Mix all ingredients together. Makes about 2 tablespoons.

The fire is the main comfort of the camp…
it is as well for cheerfulness as for warmth and dryness.

~Henry David Thoreau

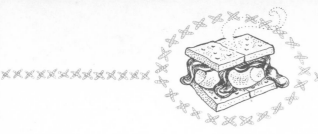

Farmhouse Dinner

Connie Bryant
Topeka, KS

When harvest season comes along, the days are busy from beginning to end. When the day's work is done, we like to settle in around a campfire and enjoy dinner together as a family.

1 lb. ground beef
4 1-oz. sticks string cheese
4 potatoes, peeled and sliced
   into 1/2-inch wedges

4 carrots, peeled and sliced
1 onion, sliced
salt and pepper to taste

Wrap 1/4 of the ground beef around each piece of cheese; arrange on 4 sheets of heavy-duty aluminum foil. Evenly divide potatoes, carrots and onion over beef; sprinkle with salt and pepper. Fold and seal edges of foil around mixture to create a packet. Place packets, seam-side down, on hot coals. Cook for 10 minutes; turn and cook for 10 additional minutes, until beef is browned and vegetables are tender. Makes 4 servings.

Pull out your oversize coffee mugs when serving soups, stews, chili, even mains and desserts 'round the campfire. They're just right for sharing hearty servings, and the handles make them so easy to hold onto.

Giovanni's Chili

Faye Mayberry
Saint David, AZ

This is a satisfying meal our family enjoys whenever we go backpacking or camping. We love to camp and a lot of our favorite memories are of these family trips. This recipe is terrific, and so easy to make.

16-oz. pkg. spaghetti, uncooked
1/2 t. salt
2 T. chili seasoning mix

2 T. taco seasoning mix
.87-oz. env. brown gravy mix
3 c. water

Measure out half the package of spaghetti and break in half; reserve the rest for another use. Combine all ingredients except water in a plastic zipping bag; shake to combine. In a soup pot or Dutch oven set on a campfire grate, bring water to a boil. Add dry ingredients from bag and cook until spaghetti is tender, about 8 to 10 minutes. Add more water if necessary to thin to desired consistency. Makes 4 servings.

Potato Soup in a Hurry

Shirley Beighley
Platteville, WI

This soup came about from much experimenting.

3 15-oz. cans diced potatoes, drained
2 14-1/2 oz. cans beef broth
10-3/4 oz. can cream of celery soup
10-3/4 oz. can cream of onion soup

16-oz. pkg. bacon, crisply cooked and diced, or
2 c. cooked, diced ham
salt and pepper to taste
Garnish: shredded cheese of your choice, diced onions

In a soup pot or Dutch oven, combine potatoes, broth and soups; stir well. Add meat and stir to blend. Place on a campfire grate over medium heat and simmer until hot, about 20 minutes. Sprinkle with salt and pepper to taste; garnish as desired. Serves 8.

Valarie's Dessert Burritos

Valarie Dennard
Palatka, FL

This is a tropical alternative to s'mores. Enjoy them at the beach,
over a campfire or even while tailgating!

4 10-inch flour tortillas
2 c. mini marshmallows
8-oz. can crushed pineapple,
   drained

1/4 c. sweetened flaked
   coconut

Arrange tortillas on separate sheets of aluminum foil. Divide
marshmallows, pineapple and coconut down the center of each
tortilla. Fold bottom third of each tortilla over filling, fold one side
in toward center, and then fold the top over. Fold and seal edges
of foil around tortilla and bake on a campfire grate over medium
coals for 7 to 10 minutes. Makes 4 servings.

Pineapple Doughnut Dessert

Debi DeVore
Dover, OH

We make these on the grill at home, but we've also enjoyed them
when camping. Kids enjoy helping make these yummy treats.

5 cake doughnuts
3 T. butter, softened
2/3 c. brown sugar, packed

20-oz. can sliced pineapple,
   drained
10 maraschino cherries

Slice doughnuts in half horizontally; spread cut sides with butter.
Arrange 2 doughnut halves, cut-side up, on a sheet of heavy-duty
aluminum foil. Sprinkle each with one tablespoon brown sugar, top
with a pineapple slice and place a cherry in the center. Seal foil
tightly. Place on a campfire grate and cook over medium heat for
3 to 5 minutes, or until heated through. Makes 10 servings.

Vivian's Chocolate Ghosts

Vivian Arledge
Edmond, OK

I created this recipe around the campfire. It is simple but oh-so-good! We like it even better than s'mores.

12 marshmallows
1.55-oz. chocolate candy bar, sectioned

Roast marshmallows over a fire until golden. Remove from stick; press a marshmallow around one chocolate section. Makes 12.

Campfire Cakes

Tara Horton
Gooseberry Patch

We had fun making these on our backyard grill, using a spoon to eat the warm cake right out of the shell! Experiment with other cake or muffin mix varieties to invent new flavor combinations.

6 oranges   9-oz. pkg. chocolate muffin mix

Cut a one to 2-inch slice off the top of each orange and set aside. Use a grapefruit spoon to hollow out the shell, being careful not to cut through the skin. Prepare muffin mix according to package instructions using water; don't add egg or oil. Fill each shell 1/2 full of cake batter; replace tops and wrap each orange in aluminum foil. Bake in hot coals, turning often, or on a grill over medium heat for 15 to 20 minutes. Let cool slightly. Makes 6 servings.

Try roasting an apple, peach or pear over the fire until tender, then dust with a bit of cinnamon-sugar!

Smoky Grilled Corn

Mary Ann Dell
Phoenixville, PA

You'll find smoked paprika in the spice aisle at your grocery.

8 ears corn, husked
4 T. olive oil, divided
1 T. kosher salt, divided

1 T. pepper, divided
1 T. smoked paprika, divided

Divide corn between 2 large plastic zipping bags. Add 2 tablespoons oil, 1/2 tablespoon salt, 1/2 tablespoon pepper and 1/2 tablespoon paprika to each bag. Close bags and gently toss to coat corn. Remove corn from bags; arrange on a campfire grate or grill over medium-high heat. Grill corn, turning often, until lightly golden, about 25 minutes. Makes 8 servings.

Grilled Ham & Potato Packet

Molly Bishop
McClure, PA

I found this recipe while searching for something to do with leftover ham. I changed a few things to suit my family's tastes, and they loved it!

5 redskin potatoes, cubed
1 onion, chopped
1 green pepper, chopped
1/2 t. salt

1-1/2 t. pepper
2-1/2 c. cooked ham, cubed
8-oz. pkg. shredded Cheddar
  cheese

Combine potatoes, onion, green pepper, salt and pepper. Stir gently to combine. Place mixture in the center of a large sheet of heavy-duty aluminum foil. Fold and seal edges of foil around mixture to create a packet. Place packet on a campfire grate or grill and cook, covered, for 20 minutes over medium heat. When potatoes are tender, carefully remove packet from grill, open and add ham cubes; stir slightly. Reseal packet and return to grill for 10 minutes. Remove packet and add cheese. Loosely close packet; return to heat for 5 minutes until cheese is melted. Serves 4.

HOMESPUN Halloween

Mom's Favorite Doughnuts

Brenda Huey
Geneva, IN

These yummy treats start with biscuit dough and are so simple
to make. I always take them to our family gatherings.

2 12-oz. tubes refrigerated
   biscuits
oil for frying

2 c. powdered sugar
2 to 3 T. water
black and orange food coloring

Using a thimble, remove the center of each biscuit; set aside. Pour
1/2 inch of oil into a deep skillet over medium-high heat. Fry
biscuits and holes in hot oil until lightly golden, about 30 seconds.
Turn and cook on second side; drain on paper towels. Let cool
completely. Combine powdered sugar and enough water to make
a glaze; divide between 2 bowls and tint with different food
coloring. Dip tops of doughnuts in glaze. Makes 20.

Spicy Pumpkin Warm-Up

Andrea Heyart
Aubrey, TX

I created this recipe a few years ago and it has quickly become a fall
tradition in our home. Try serving it either hot or cold in glasses
rimmed with graham cracker crumbs for a fun party drink!

2 pts. whipping cream
1/2 c. sugar
1/3 c. canned pumpkin
1 t. pumpkin pie spice

1/2 t. vanilla extract
Garnish: whipped cream,
   additional pumpkin pie spice

Combine cream and sugar in a saucepan over medium heat; stir
until sugar is dissolved. Whisk in pumpkin until well blended; add
pumpkin pie spice and vanilla. Simmer for 10 to 15 minutes, or until
mixture is warm. Pour into mugs and serve with a dollop of whipped
cream and a sprinkle of spice. Serves 4 to 6.

Spooky-Sweet Candy Corn

Laura Fuller
Fort Wayne, IN

This autumn treat is super-simple to make at home.

1 c. sugar
1/3 c. butter
2/3 c. light corn syrup
1 t. vanilla extract

2-1/2 c. powdered sugar
1/4 t. salt
1/3 c. powdered milk
red and yellow food coloring

Combine sugar, butter and corn syrup in a heavy saucepan over medium heat. Bring to a boil, stirring constantly. Reduce heat to low and boil 5 minutes, stirring occasionally. Remove from heat and add vanilla; set aside. Combine powdered sugar, salt and powdered milk; stir into sugar mixture. Let stand about 20 minutes, or until cool enough to handle. Divide dough into 3 equal parts and place in bowls. Wearing plastic gloves, knead desired amount of yellow food coloring into one bowl of dough; knead desired amount of yellow and red into the second bowl to create orange. Leave remaining bowl uncolored. Roll each portion of dough into a long, thin rope of equal lengths. Arrange dough ropes side-by-side; press seams together using a rolling pin. Cut into triangles with a sharp knife; shape edges to resemble corn kernels. Set aside until firm; store in an airtight container. Makes about one pound.

Slide a long length of kitchen twine through the holes in glazed doughnuts, then hang them from tree branches. With hands held behind backs, who can catch and eat a doughnut first?

Wizard Hats

Beth Kramer
Port Saint Lucie, FL

I took these to my son's kindergarten class and they were a hit!

3 c. puffed rice cereal
1-oz. sq. unsweetened baking
  chocolate
1 c. mini marshmallows

3 T. corn syrup
12-oz. pkg. semi-sweet
  chocolate chips
Garnish: candy sprinkles

Pour cereal into a shallow pan; bake at 350 degrees 10 minutes. Transfer to a bowl lightly coated with non-stick vegetable spray; set aside. Meanwhile, in a saucepan over low heat, combine chocolate and marshmallows; cook and stir until melted. Add corn syrup; stir well. Pour chocolate mixture over cereal; stir to coat cereal evenly. Divide mixture into 8 portions; shape each into a cone. Add chocolate chips to the top of a double boiler over boiling water; melt chocolate, stirring occasionally. Dip cones into melted chocolate, turning to coat. Place on wax paper; garnish with sprinkles; cool. Makes 8.

A super-simple idea…insert all flavors of lollipops into a foam pumpkin for a clever lollipop holder. Don't be tempted to use a real pumpkin, the moisture inside will make the lollipop sticks soggy.

Chocolate Witch Cauldrons

Sheila Kluesener
West Chester, OH

Top these adorable "cauldrons" with gummy worms for a real treat!

24 chocolate sandwich cookies,
  crushed
1/2 c. butter, melted
1 c. milk
3/4 c. whipping cream
3.3-oz. pkg. instant white
  chocolate pudding mix

10 drops green food coloring
1/2 c. semi-sweet mini
  chocolate chips
12 pretzel sticks

Place foil baking cups in each of 12 muffin cups; set aside.
Combine cookie crumbs and melted butter in a bowl; stir to mix.
Spoon 2 heaping tablespoonfuls into each baking cup; press into
the bottom and up the sides. Using an electric mixer on high speed,
beat together milk, whipping cream, pudding mix and coloring for
one minute; stir in chocolate chips. Spoon pudding mixture into
prepared muffin cups. Chill one hour. Before serving, place a pretzel
stick into each "cauldron." Makes 12.

When the autumn weather is just right, a backyard
treasure hunt is a great party activity. Hide stickers,
wrapped candies and small toys like spider rings.

Bewitching Spinach Dip

Lisa Johnson
Hallsville, TX

When I was teaching, once a month we'd all bring one of our favorites to school for our lunch...this dip was always a hit! I'd always have to make a double batch, to make sure there was enough for everyone.

3 to 4 green onions
1/2 c. fresh parsley
10-oz. pkg. frozen chopped
   spinach, slightly thawed
8-oz. pkg. cream cheese,
   softened
3 T. dried, minced onion
1 c. cottage cheese

1 c. mayonnaise
1/2 c. sour cream
1/4 t. hot pepper sauce
1/4 t. pepper
1/4 c. lemon juice
assorted crackers, cut-up
   vegetables

Combine green onions and parsley in a food processor; pulse to chop. Add spinach and continue to process until spinach has been finely chopped. Remove from processor and set aside. Without rinsing the processor, add remaining ingredients except crackers and vegetables. Blend until well mixed. Stir into spinach mixture, blending well. Spoon into a serving bowl; chill several hours before serving. Serve with crackers and vegetables. Makes about 8 cups.

Serve up mummy dogs in a jiffy. Simply wrap a strip
of breadstick dough around individual hot dogs.
Arrange them on an ungreased baking sheet and
bake at 375 degrees for 12 to 15 minutes.

Sloppy Goblins

Beth Bundy
Long Prairie, MN

*I'm a busy mom and often look for fast recipes. With only
5 ingredients, these yummy Sloppy Joes couldn't be easier!*

1 lb. ground beef
1/2 c. onion, diced
10-3/4 oz. can chicken
   gumbo soup

3 T. catsup
1 T. mustard
8 hamburger buns, split
   and toasted

Brown beef and onion in a skillet over medium heat; drain. Stir in
soup, catsup and mustard. Simmer 30 minutes; spoon onto warm
buns. Serves 8.

Make spooky sandwiches for Halloween night!
Slice pimento-stuffed green olives for eyes, add a
banana pepper nose and carrot crinkles for a mouth.

Mummy Fingers

Carla Jones
Weatherford, TX

*Not really, but these chicken fingers do make a quick dinner before
sending out kids for trick-or-treating. There's no need to
turn the chicken, it always comes out moist and tender.*

7 saltine crackers
2 T. grated Parmesan cheese
1/8 t. garlic powder

8 chicken tenders
1/2 c. Italian salad dressing

Place crackers, cheese and garlic in a blender or food processor;
blend until crumbly. Dip chicken in Italian dressing; roll in cracker
mixture. Arrange on a lightly greased baking sheet and bake at
350 degrees for 20 minutes. Serves 3 to 4.

A side of potato bugs is nice with any Halloween dinner!
Bake frozen potato puffs on lightly greased baking sheets
at 375 degrees for 7 minutes. Slide 3 puffs onto a dry piece
of spaghetti; return to oven and bake 5 minutes longer.
Give each section legs using thin strips of carrots,
then add dots of catsup for eyes.

Poisoned Rice

Kathy Dassel
Newburgh, IN

My sister-in-law gave me this recipe while we were visiting her in Raleigh, North Carolina, and I made it often when we returned home. My nieces were small at the time and were a bit afraid to eat it because of the wacky name, so we called it Aunt Kathy's Rice Casserole for quite awhile. They both grew to love it, so we all call it by its original name now!

4-oz. can sliced mushrooms, drained and liquid reserved
8-oz. can sliced water chestnuts, drained and liquid reserved

1/2 c. butter
1 c. long-cooking rice, uncooked
10-1/2 oz. can French onion soup

In a skillet over medium heat, sauté mushrooms and water chestnuts in butter. Set aside. Add rice to an ungreased one-quart casserole dish. Stir in soup, mushroom mixture and reserved liquids. Bake, covered, at 375 degrees for 45 to 60 minutes. Serves 6 to 8.

Creepy, Crawly Corn

Samantha Moyer
Farragut, IA

This is such a family favorite, that at the end of the meal, everyone wants to take home the leftovers!

15-1/4 oz. can corn
14-3/4 oz. can creamed corn
1/2 c. margarine, melted
1 c. pasteurized process cheese, cubed

1 c. spaghetti, uncooked and broken

Combine undrained corn and remaining ingredients in a greased 2-quart casserole dish. Bake, uncovered, at 325 degrees for one hour, stirring halfway through baking time. Serves 6.

Grandmother's Punch

Brooke Busby
Somerset, KY

My grandmother makes this punch for holiday gatherings, birthday parties and family get-togethers. She passed the recipe on to me and now I make it every chance I get. Kids and adults just love it!

6-oz. pkg. cherry gelatin mix
2 c. sugar
4 c. boiling water
3/4 c. frozen lemonade
    concentrate

48-oz. can pineapple juice
4-1/2 c. cold water
1 to 2 2-ltr. bottles lemon-lime
    soda, chilled

Stir gelatin mix and sugar into boiling water until completely dissolved. Add lemonade and pineapple juice; mix well. Blend in cold water. Pour mixture into gallon-size plastic freezer bags; freeze overnight. Remove bags from the freezer 2 hours before serving; knead slightly while in bag. Place mixture in a punch bowl, adding desired amount of soda. Serves 45.

Serve up frosty punch in boo-tiful glasses. Place 1/3 cup of chocolate chips in a microwave-safe bowl; microwave on high until chips melt. Using a small artist's brush, paint a mouth and eyes inside punch glasses. Let set a few minutes to harden, fill with punch and serve immediately.

Black Kitty Kat Cupcakes

Mildred Biggin
Lyons, IL

Don't be afraid of these black cats, they are devilishly good!

18-1/2 oz. pkg. devil's food
   cake mix
12 chocolate sandwich cookies,
   quartered
16-oz. can dark chocolate
   frosting

48 yellow or green jellybeans
24 black jellybeans
24 pieces black rope licorice

Prepare and bake cake according to package directions for cupcakes using paper liners. Cool for 10 minutes, then remove and place on wire racks to cool completely. Frost tops of cupcakes; insert 2 cookie pieces for ears and lightly frost each. Arrange yellow or green jellybeans for eyes and a black jellybean for the nose. Cut each piece of black licorice into thirds, then in half. Place 3 halves on each side of the nose for whiskers. Makes 2 dozen.

Whip up a chocolatey homemade buttercream frosting
in no time. Beat together 6 tablespoons butter with
2-2/3 cups powdered sugar, 1/2 cup baking cocoa,
4 to 6 tablespoons milk and one teaspoon vanilla extract.
This makes about 2 cups of the yummiest frosting
for spreading on cupcakes or cookies.

Boo-tiful Pumpkin Cake

Jennifer Inacio
Hummelstown, PA

My son requests this as soon as it gets close to Halloween...it's become our tradition. If you make 2 of these in Bundt® pans, you can put them together to make a fun pumpkin cake! Just put one cake upside-down on a plate, then top with another cake right-side up and frost with orange-tinted frosting.

4 eggs, beaten	2 c. all-purpose flour
2 c. sugar	1 t. salt
1 c. oil	2 t. baking soda
15-oz. can pumpkin	1-1/2 t. cinnamon

Combine eggs, sugar and oil in a large bowl; beat with an electric mixer on high speed until mixture is lemon-colored and thick. Blend in pumpkin; set aside. In another bowl, whisk together flour, salt, baking soda and cinnamon. Add 1/2 cup at a time to the pumpkin mixture, blending well after each addition. Pour batter into a lightly greased 13"x9" baking pan and bake at 350 degrees for 40 minutes, or until a toothpick comes out clean. If using a Bundt® pan, bake for 30 minutes at 350 degrees, then reduce temperature to 325 degrees for an additional 20 to 25 minutes. Check for doneness. Cool completely before frosting. Serves 8 to 10.

Cream Cheese Frosting:

8-oz. pkg. cream cheese, softened	1 t. vanilla extract
1/4 c. butter, softened	1-1/2 to 2 c. powdered sugar
	2 to 3 T. milk

Blend cream cheese, butter and vanilla together. Stir in as much powdered sugar and milk as needed to achieve desired consistency.

Haunt your house with eerie music...your local library
will have lots of CDs to choose from!

Monster Munch

*Katie Majeske
Denver, PA*

You can use any combination of your favorite crunchy cereal or small crackers in this recipe. I have packaged this in small containers and sent it to college students as a tasty treat.

9 c. cereal or small crackers
  of your choice
4 c. popped popcorn
1-1/2 c. dry roasted peanuts
1 c. brown sugar, packed

1/2 c. butter
1/2 c. light corn syrup
1 t. vanilla extract
1/2 t. baking soda
2 c. candy-coated chocolates

Lightly grease a large roasting pan; stir in cereal or crackers, popcorn and peanuts. In a saucepan over medium heat, mix brown sugar, butter and corn syrup. Bring to a boil and cook, without stirring, for 5 minutes. Remove from heat; add vanilla and baking soda. Mix well and pour over mixture in roasting pan; toss to coat. Bake at 250 degrees for 45 minutes, stirring every 15 minutes. Cool completely; add candy, tossing to mix. Store in an airtight container. Makes 12 to 16 servings.

Give scoops of snack mix inside a witch's broom...what a clever party favor! Fill sandwich-size plastic zipping bags with snack mix, then tuck a bag inside a crumpled brown paper lunch sack. Slip a pretzel rod inside, gathering the bag around it. Tie the bag closed with a string of black licorice.

Cinna-Mocha Mix

Barb Henderson
Everton, AR

This is great for those brisk mornings…it warms you to your toes.

1-3/4 c. powdered non-dairy
  creamer
3/4 c. sugar
1/2 c. baking cocoa
1/3 c. instant coffee granules

1/4 c. brown sugar, packed
1 t. cinnamon
1/4 t. salt
1/4 t. nutmeg

Place all ingredients in a blender or food processor and pulse until finely ground. Store in an airtight container. To serve, stir 1/4 cup mix into 3/4 cup boiling water. Makes 14 servings.

Toxic Waste Punch

Carey Neblett
Pleasant View, TN

Halloween is my family's favorite holiday. We have a huge party every year, so I like to try and "wow" everyone with my food and decorations. This punch is a winner!

2 c. sugar
2 qts. water
2 .1-oz envs. unsweetened
  lime drink mix

46-oz. can pineapple juice
4 c. ginger ale, chilled
Garnish: glow sticks,
  plastic bugs

Stir all ingredients together except ginger ale and garnish. Blend well to dissolve sugar. Pour into a punch bowl or plastic cauldron and slowly add ginger ale. Stir to blend. Surround punch bowl with glow sticks and plastic bugs. Makes 15 servings.

Monstrously Good Cookies

Joyce LaMure
Sequim, WA

I received this recipe from my neighbor over 26 years ago and have since made it for our son as a tasty after-school snack. It makes a lot of cookies...great for all those Halloween and harvest parties, or you can simply freeze any leftover dough for later use.

2 c. margarine, softened
6-1/4 c. chunky peanut butter
2 16-oz. pkgs. brown sugar
4 c. sugar
1 T. corn syrup
1 T. vanilla extract
8 t. baking soda

1 doz. eggs, beaten
12-oz. pkg. chocolate chips
16-oz. pkg. candy-coated chocolates or candy-coated peanut butter-filled candies
18 c. quick-cooking oats, uncooked

In a very large bowl, mix ingredients in order given. Place dough by 1/4 cupfuls on ungreased baking sheets. Bake at 350 degrees for 8 to 10 minutes. Makes 12 dozen.

Greet friends and neighbors with a harvest flag garland hanging across a doorway or along a mantel. Decorate sheets of red, orange, yellow and brown construction paper with rubber stamps, glitter and paper punches. Use only black and orange paper for a clever Halloween garland! Secure each panel to a length of black string using double-sided adhesive tape.

Magic Potion Chili

Lisa Sett
Thousand Oaks, CA

This slow-cooker recipe is similar to a popular fast-food chili recipe.
We also love to serve it spooned over baked potatoes
and top with shredded cheese.

1 to 2 lbs. ground beef,
   browned and drained
4-oz. can diced green chiles
10-1/2 oz. can French onion
   soup
1 T. chili powder
21-oz. can red kidney beans,
   drained and rinsed

2 t. ground cumin
6-oz. can tomato paste
3/4 c. water
1/2 t. pepper
1/8 to 1/4 t. hot pepper sauce
Garnish: shredded Cheddar
   cheese

Add all ingredients, except garnish, to a slow cooker; stir to blend.
Cover and cook on low setting for 4 to 6 hours. Spoon into serving
bowls and garnish with cheese. Serves 6 to 8.

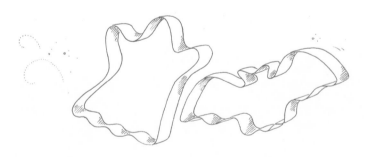

Wrap silverware in napkins, then slip a cookie cutter
over each as a clever napkin ring. You'll find all sorts of
fun fall shapes such as leaves and pumpkins. Look for
bats and ghosts during Halloween.

Ghoulish Chowder
Vickie

What are those things floating in my bowl? Oh, they're only French fried onions, but they do look like something spooky!

1 T. butter
2 t. garlic, minced
4 tomatoes, chopped
1 c. water
15-oz. can tomato sauce
1 c. frozen corn

1/4 c. fresh cilantro, chopped
1 T. hot pepper sauce
1/2 t. chili powder
Garnish: avocado slices,
   shredded Monterey Jack
   cheese, French fried onions

Melt butter in a saucepan over medium heat. Add garlic; cook and stir for one minute. Stir in tomatoes and cook for 5 minutes. Add remaining ingredients, except garnish, and bring to a boil. Reduce heat and simmer for 10 minutes. Ladle soup into bowls; garnish as desired. Serves 4.

Garnish individual servings of soup or chili with a sour cream "spiderweb." Spoon sour cream into a plastic zipping bag, then seal the bag. Snip a tiny corner from the bag and pipe sour cream in circles over the soup. Starting at the center, run the tip of a knife through the sour cream to the edge of the bowl several times to resemble a spiderweb.

Spooky Pizza Dip

Gloria Robertson
Midland, TX

Don't let the name worry you, this savory dip is the best! Serve it with toasted baguettes, English muffins or pita bread.

8-oz. pkg. cream cheese,
  softened
1 t. Italian seasoning
1 c. shredded mozzarella
  cheese
3/4 c. grated Parmesan cheese

8-oz. can pizza sauce
1/4 c. red or green pepper,
  diced
Optional: cooked sausage or
  chopped pepperoni
assorted crackers

Blend together cream cheese and seasoning; spread on the bottom of an ungreased 9"x9" baking pan. Combine cheeses and sprinkle half over cream cheese mixture. Spoon on pizza sauce, spreading to edges. Sprinkle with pepper and, if desired, sausage or pepperoni slices. Top with remaining cheese mixture. Bake at 350 degrees for 15 to 20 minutes. Serve with crackers. Serves 10 to 12.

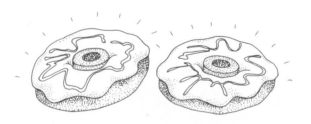

Every Halloween buffet needs some Eyes of Newt! Blend together an 8-ounce package of softened cream cheese with a clove of minced garlic. Spread about 2 tablespoons over eight, 6-inch tortillas. Roll up jelly-roll style and refrigerate one hour. Trim and discard the uneven ends, then slice the rolled tortillas into one-inch pieces. Arrange on a platter, cut-side up, and place a black olive slice on each end to resemble an eye.

Pumpkin Cheese Ball

Carey Neblett
Pleasant View, TN

I made this at my very first Halloween party...it looks just like a real pumpkin!

2 8-oz. pkgs. extra sharp
   Cheddar cheese
8-oz. pkg. cream cheese,
   softened
8-oz. container chive and onion
   cream cheese, softened

2 t. paprika
1/2 t. cayenne pepper
1 stalk broccoli, top removed
assorted crackers

Combine all ingredients except broccoli and crackers. Shape mixture to resemble a pumpkin. Trim broccoli stalk, if needed, and press lightly into the top of the pumpkin for a stem. Use a knife to make vertical lines down the sides of the cheese ball. Serve with crackers. Serves 10 to 15.

Vanishing Pretzels

Patricia Wissler
Harrisburg, PA

These are so very good and so easy to make...they disappear in no time at all! They're always a hit whenever I serve them.

12-oz. bag mini pretzel twists
1/4 c. butter

1/4 t. garlic powder
1/4 c. grated Parmesan cheese

Place pretzels in a large microwave-safe bowl; set aside. Combine butter and garlic powder in a one-cup glass measuring cup. Microwave on high setting 30 to 45 seconds; stir to combine. Drizzle mixture over pretzels and lightly toss. Sprinkle with cheese; toss again. Microwave on high setting 3 to 4 minutes, stirring once or twice. Cool; store in a tightly covered container. Serves 12.

Frightfully Good Chicken

Sherri Robinson
McMinnville, OR

I created this yummy chicken recipe for my slow cooker on a day it was too snowy to get to the store. I went through my pantry and just tossed the ingredients in the slow cooker. It ended up being the most flavorful and moist chicken we have ever tasted!

4 to 6 boneless, skinless
    chicken breasts
1 to 2 10-1/2 oz. cans chicken
    broth

1 to 2 c. barbecue sauce

Spray a slow cooker with non-stick butter-flavored vegetable spray. Arrange chicken breasts in slow cooker; add enough broth to almost cover chicken. Add enough sauce to completely cover chicken. Cover and cook on low setting for 5 to 6 hours. Serves 4 to 6.

For a fresh spin on decorated pumpkins, lightly coat
a white Lumina pumpkin with spray adhesive,
then dust with fine sparkly glitter.

Mac & Cheese, Please

*Kristie Rigo
Friedens, PA*

*This slow-cooker macaroni & cheese is so easy and delicious!
The cayenne pepper kicks up the flavor, but to get a completely
different taste, add canned green chiles and chili powder.*

8-oz. pkg. elbow macaroni,
   cooked
12-oz. can evaporated milk
1 c. milk
1/4 c. butter, melted and
   slightly cooled

2 eggs, beaten
4 c. shredded Cheddar cheese,
   divided
salt and pepper to taste
1/2 t. cayenne pepper
1/4 c. grated Parmesan cheese

Combine macaroni, milks, butter, eggs, 3 cups Cheddar cheese, salt
and pepper. Top with remaining Cheddar and Parmesan. Cover and
cook on low setting for 3 hours. Serves 4.

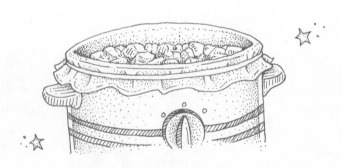

Don't miss a bit of the harvest fun! Line your slow cooker
with special plastic liners designed just for slow cooking.
They make clean-up a breeze…simply lift out,
remove prepared food and toss the liner.

Halloween Party Mix

Brenda Huey
Geneva, IN

*I put this mix into bags, tie with pretty Halloween ribbon
and give to little trick-or-treaters.*

2 c. candy-coated peanut
   butter-filled candies
2 c. doughnut-shaped oat cereal
2 c. candy corn
2 c. honeycomb-shaped corn
   and oat cereal

2 c. salted peanuts
2 c. bagel chips
2 c. bite-size crispy rice cereal
   squares

Toss all ingredients together. Store in an airtight container. Makes
14 cups.

Trick-or-Treat Trifle

Irene Whatling
West Des Moines, IA

Use your favorite candy bars for this easy recipe.

18-1/2 oz. pkg. chocolate
   cake mix
5.9-oz. pkg. instant chocolate
   pudding mix

2 1.4-oz. chocolate-covered
   toffee candy bars, chopped
16-oz. container frozen
   whipped topping, thawed

Prepare and bake cake mix according to package directions. Cool
and cut into large pieces. Prepare pudding mix according to package
directions; set aside. In a large, deep bowl, layer ingredients
beginning with half each of the cake, pudding, whipped topping
and candy bar pieces. Repeat layering again in the same order;
cover and refrigerate overnight. Serves 10 to 12.

Enjoy an old-fashioned cake walk at your next harvest
get-together. What fun!

HARVEST
Pantry

Strawberry Jam

Cherries

Apple Butt

Pe
Sau

Strawberry-Orange Jam

Lorrie Smith
Drummonds, TN

*My grandmother made this jam when I was young, and she always
used quilted crystal jelly jars. I remember eating it
spread on warm biscuits...mmm!*

1 orange, peeled and seeded
2 10-oz. pkgs. frozen
   strawberries, thawed
1/4 c. water

2 T. powdered pectin
3-1/2 c. sugar
4 to 5 1/2-pint canning jars
   and lids, sterilized

In a food processor, grind orange using a fine blade. Combine
strawberries, orange and water in a large kettle; stir in pectin.
Over high heat, bring mixture to a rolling boil, stirring constantly.
Add sugar and continue stirring. Return to a rolling boil and boil
one minute, stirring constantly. Remove from heat; skim foam if
needed and stir well. Spoon into hot sterilized jars, leaving
1/4-inch headspace. Wipe rims and secure lids and rings. Process
in a boiling-water bath for 10 minutes. Set jars on a towel to cool.
Check for seals. Makes 4 to 5 jars.

Attach a cheery fabric yo-yo, quilt square or
felted wool flower to the tops of homemade
jams & jellies...such pretty jar toppers!

Blueberry-Lemon Jam

Cindy Smith
Cumming, GA

*Our family took a trip to pick blueberries and came home
with so many! This was the recipe I turned to,
and the resulting jam was delicious.*

4-1/2 c. blueberries
6-1/2 c. sugar
juice and zest of 2 lemons

2 3-oz. pkgs. liquid pectin
7 1/2-pint canning jars and
  lids, sterilized

Combine blueberries, sugar, lemon juice and zest in a large saucepan
over high heat; bring to a boil. Stir in pectin; bring to a rolling boil
and stir constantly for one minute. Remove from heat; skim foam
if needed. Spoon into hot sterilized jars, leaving 1/4-inch headspace.
Wipe rims and secure lids and rings. Process in a boiling-water
bath for 15 minutes. Set jars on a towel to cool. Check for seals.
Makes 7 jars.

Sharing Mom's and Grandma's tried & true canning
recipes is a great way to hand down favorite recipes that
generations have loved. Keep the recipes, but be sure
to update the preserving methods if needed. Some ways
Grandma canned, using a wax seal or the inversion
method for jams & jellies, are no longer a good
way to keep foods their freshest.

Nutty Pumpkin Butter

Abigail Smith
Gooseberry Patch

A jar of this yummy butter will be a welcome gift for friends & family.
Give jars tucked into a basket with warm buttermilk biscuits.

3-1/2 c. canned pumpkin
1 c. pecans, toasted and
   chopped
1 T. pumpkin pie spice
1-3/4 oz. pkg. powdered pectin

1/2 t. margarine
4-1/2 c. sugar
5 1/2-pint canning jars and
   lids, sterilized

Combine pumpkin, pecans and spice in a large saucepan; stir in
pectin. Add margarine and bring to a boil over high heat, stirring
constantly. Quickly add sugar; stir to dissolve. Boil for one minute,
stirring constantly. Remove from heat; skim off foam if needed. Spoon
into hot sterilized jars, leaving 1/4-inch headspace. Wipe rims and
secure lids and rings. Process in a boiling water-bath for 15 minutes.
Set jars on a towel to cool. Check for seals. Makes 5 jars.

Enter your preserves, jams, jellies
or pickles in your local county fair.
You just may be surprised at how
well you do!

Slow-Cooker Apple Butter

Judith Jennings
Ironwood, MI

A fall trip to the orchard will send you home with baskets of the best, crunchy apples. While lots of them become scrumptious pies, don't miss the chance to turn them into this wonderful apple butter.

12 Granny Smith apples, cored,
  peeled and quartered
1-1/2 c. brown sugar, packed
1/2 c. apple juice
1 T. lemon juice

1 t. allspice
4 1/2-pint freezer-safe
  plastic containers and lids,
  sterilized

Combine all ingredients in a slow cooker. Cover and cook on low setting for 8 to 10 hours, or until apples are very tender. Mash apples with potato masher or fork. Cook, uncovered, on low setting for one to 2 hours, stirring occasionally, until mixture is very thick. Cool about 2 hours. Spoon into sterilized containers, leaving 1/2-inch headspace; secure lids and freeze. Thaw in refrigerator before using. Makes 4 containers.

Get together with friends for a day of pickling and preserving! Tie on your prettiest aprons and catch up on what's new. Then stand back and smile at all the delicious foods your family will enjoy all winter long.

Pike Family Jalapeño Jelly

Diana Pike
Mount Vernon, OH

This is the best hot pepper jelly I have ever tried...it's an essential treat around the holidays! Our family serves it on whole-wheat crackers with a bit of cream cheese. So pretty and so good!

3/4 c. green pepper, chopped
1/4 c. jalapeño pepper, chopped
6 c. sugar
1-1/2 c. cider vinegar

1/2 c. liquid pectin
4 drops green food coloring
6 1/2-pint canning jars
  and lids

Add peppers to a food processor and pulse until finely minced. Combine pepper mixture, sugar and vinegar in a saucepan over medium-high heat; bring to a rolling boil. Remove from heat; stir in pectin and food coloring. Ladle jelly into sterilized jars, leaving 1/2-inch headspace. Wipe rims and secure lids and rings. Process in a boiling-water bath for 5 minutes. Set jars on a towel to cool. Check for seals. Makes 6 containers.

Gather all your fun scrapbooking supplies and easily make the prettiest jar labels. Buttons, stickers, die-cuts, rick rack and decorative-edge scissors are all you need for whimsical, one-of-a-kind labels and tags!

All-Around Pasta Sauce

*Mary Murray
Mount Vernon, OH*

*A sauce that's good on everything from
spaghetti to lasagna to ravioli.*

2 onions, chopped
2 cloves garlic, minced
2 T. olive oil
2 14-1/2 oz. cans diced
   tomatoes with basil, garlic
   and oregano
2 12-oz. cans tomato paste
6 c. tomatoes, chopped

3 T. dark brown sugar, packed
3 T. fresh oregano, snipped
3 T. fresh basil, snipped
salt and pepper to taste
2 1-qt. freezer-safe plastic
   containers and lids,
   sterilized

Sauté onions and garlic in oil in a large stockpot over medium heat.
Add remaining ingredients; bring to a boil. Reduce heat to low and
simmer, partially covered, for one to 2 hours, stirring occasionally,
until desired thickness is reached. Cool to warm; spoon into freezer
containers, leaving 1/2-inch headspace. Secure lids and freeze.
Makes 2 containers.

If you find yourself with more tomatoes than you have
time to prepare for sauce, turn them into tomato juice!
Simply cut tomatoes into quarters and simmer 10 minutes.
Strain and add one teaspoon salt to each quart of juice.
Pour the juice into freezer-safe plastic containers, leaving
1/2-inch headspace. Seal, then freeze. Perfect for any
recipe that calls for tomato juice.

Sizzlin' Butter

Staci Meyers
Montezuma, GA

A real family favorite, we like to use hot Hungarian wax peppers.
This is great for dipping pretzels into or spreading on sandwiches.
Try spreading over ham, steaks or chicken before cooking…yum!

36 hot banana peppers, seeded
   and chopped
4 c. white or cider vinegar,
   divided
1 T. salt
4 c. mustard

5 to 6 c. sugar
1-1/2 c. all-purpose flour
1 c. cold water
8 1-pint canning jars and lids,
   sterilized

Combine peppers and one cup vinegar in a food processor or
blender; process until smooth. In a large stockpot, combine pepper
mixture, remaining vinegar, salt, mustard and sugar. Cook over
medium-high heat, stirring often, until mixture thickens, about
15 minutes. Stir flour and cold water together to make a thin paste;
mix until smooth. Pour over pepper mixture and bring to a boil.
Stirring constantly, cook for 10 minutes. Spoon into hot sterilized
jars, leaving 1/4-inch headspace. Wipe rims and secure lids and
rings. Process in a boiling-water bath for 5 minutes. Set jars on a
towel to cool. Check for seals. Makes 8 jars.

Bruschetta is a quick & easy recipe and tastes amazing
with tomatoes still warm from the sun and fresh basil.
Dice 4 tomatoes and mix with 2 teaspoons olive oil and
one teaspoon freshly chopped basil. Spread over
toasted slices of Italian bread. Yum!

Amish Hot Pepper Rings

Cyndy DeStefano
Mercer, PA

We love summer for many reasons but one of the best things is the Amish produce stand that opens right down the road from us. Our Amish neighbor taught me how to can peppers several different ways, but these are by far our favorite! We enjoy them on just about everything, from tortilla chips and pizza to sandwiches and steaks.

2 T. lemon pepper
1 T. salt
1 T. garlic powder
1 T. onion powder
1 c. vegetable oil
1 c. olive oil
2 c. vinegar
2-1/2 c. sugar

12-oz. can tomato paste
12 lbs. sweet peppers, seeded
  and sliced
13 lbs. hot peppers, seeded
  and sliced
8 1-pint canning jars and lids,
  sterilized

Combine all ingredients except peppers in a very large stockpot; bring to a boil. Turn off heat and add pepper rings. Set aside for 20 minutes, stirring occasionally. Spoon into hot sterilized jars, leaving 1/4-inch headspace. Wipe rims and secure lids and rings. Process in a boiling-water bath for 20 minutes. Set jars on a towel to cool. Check for seals. Makes 8 jars.

It seems like we all have some of Mom's or Grandma's favorite handwritten recipes on well-worn recipe cards. Invite your family to send you copies of recipe cards they have, then put together a family cookbook to share. There's something so sweet about all those tried & true recipes in her original handwriting.

Sweet Freezer Slaw

Nellie Burskey
Pittsburgh, PA

A classic recipe that's easy and delicious. You'll love the taste and its make-ahead convenience!

1 head cabbage, shredded
1 carrot, peeled and shredded
1 green pepper, finely diced
2 T. pickling salt
1 c. cider vinegar
1-1/4 c. sugar

1/4 c. water
1 t. celery seed
4 1-pint freezer-safe plastic
   containers and lids,
   sterilized

Combine cabbage, carrot and pepper; sprinkle with salt and mix well. Set aside, covered, for one hour. Meanwhile, combine vinegar, sugar, water and celery seed in a saucepan over medium-high heat. Bring to a boil; boil one minute. Rinse vegetables in cold water; drain and squeeze out remaining water. Pour hot mixture over vegetables; stir well and set aside to cool. Pack in freezer-safe containers, leaving 1/2-inch headspace. Secure lids and freeze. Thaw in refrigerator before serving. Makes 4 containers.

You can preserve your bounty of harvest herbs too.
Gently rinse and place them in a single layer in a
dehydrator set at 110 degrees. Herbs such as cilantro,
dill, fennel, mint, parsley, rosemary, savory, tarragon and
thyme will take 6 to 8 hours to dry. Other herbs like
basil and sage will take longer, about 10 to 12 hours.

Just Peachy Freezer Jam

Sherry Gordon
Arlington Heights, IL

I absolutely love the taste of summertime peaches, and this jam lets me enjoy that sweet flavor even when it's snowing outside!

3 c. peaches, pitted, peeled
   and finely chopped
4-1/2 c. sugar
2 T. lemon juice
3/4 c. water

1-3/4 oz. pkg. powdered
   pectin
6 1/2-pint freezer-safe
   plastic containers and lids,
   sterilized

Combine peaches, sugar and lemon juice in a large bowl; set aside 10 minutes, stirring occasionally. Mix water and pectin in a saucepan. Bring to a boil over high heat, stirring constantly. Continue boiling and stirring one minute; add to peach mixture, stirring until sugar is dissolved. Spoon into sterilized containers, leaving 1/2-inch headspace; secure lids. Let stand at room temperature 24 hours. Jam is now ready to freeze. Thaw in refrigerator before using. Makes 6 containers.

If you just can't wait, enjoy freezer jams, jellies or pickles without freezing…they'll stay fresh in the refrigerator for about 3 weeks.

Mom's Pickled Corn

Sharon Tillman
Hampton, VA

A yummy sweet-tart twist on an old favorite. You'll love serving it alongside fresh veggies and dip or with a relish platter.

6 ears corn, husked and
   quartered
1 T. salt
3 c. white vinegar
1 c. sugar

1 T. mixed pickling spice
2 bay leaves
3-inch cinnamon stick
2 1-quart canning jars and
   lids, sterilized

Place corn in a large bowl. Sprinkle with salt and add enough water to cover. Refrigerate, covered. Combine vinegar, sugar, pickling spice, bay leaves and cinnamon stick in a stockpot. Bring to a boil over medium heat, stirring occasionally until sugar has dissolved. Drain and rinse corn with cold water; place into stockpot with pickling mixture. Bring to a boil over high heat, then reduce heat to low and simmer 10 minutes. Remove corn with a slotted spoon and divide between hot sterilized jars. Remove cinnamon stick and bay leaves from liquid; discard. Spoon vinegar mixture from stockpot into jars, completely covering corn. Leave 1/4-inch headspace. Wipe rims and secure lids and rings. Process in a boiling-water bath for 10 minutes. Set jars on a towel to cool. Check for seals. Makes 2 jars.

Here's a super tip for easily removing corn kernels
from the cob. Set an ear of corn in the center opening
of an angel food cake pan and run a sharp knife
down the ear...the kernels will slide right into
the pan when sliced from the cob!

Dilly Green Beans

Kerry Mayer
Dunham Springs, LA

This is a recipe I remember my grandmother preparing each harvest season. Her pantry shelves would be lined up with jars of these beans, tomatoes, bread & butter pickles and hot peppers.

3-1/2 c. white vinegar
3 c. water
3 T. kosher salt
1/4 c. sugar
1 onion, cut into 6 1/4-inch
   slices
36 whole black peppercorns
18 whole green peppercorns
1/4 t. mustard seed
1/4 t. dill seed
6 bay leaves
4 lbs. green beans, trimmed
   and cut into 4-inch pieces

6 small serrano chiles, rinsed
   and stems removed
6 baby carrots, halved
   lengthwise
6 cloves garlic, peeled and
   halved
3 bunches fresh dill, stemmed
1 lemon, cut into 6 1/8-inch
   slices and seeded
6 1-pint canning jars and lids,
   sterilized

Combine vinegar, water, salt and sugar in a large saucepan; bring to a boil over high heat. Reduce heat and simmer while packing jars. Place an onion slice, spices and one bay leaf in the bottom of each jar. Pack green beans, chiles, carrots and garlic tightly into jars. Place fresh dill on top, tucking in so none touches the rim. Top each jar with a lemon slice to hold down dill. Spoon boiling vinegar mixture into jars, leaving 1/4-inch headspace. Make sure all of the dill is tucked in. Wipe rims and secure lids and rings. Process in a boiling-water bath for 10 minutes. Set jars on a towel to cool. Check for seals. Allow to set for at least 3 weeks before using. Makes 6 jars.

Invite a friend over who wants to learn to preserve food and share your best recipes with her. She'll save money and enjoy the homegrown flavor of foods all winter long, and you'll be passing along tried & true recipes for another family to enjoy.

Apple Pie Filling

Rhoda Rine
Mount Vernon, OH

This is the best pie filling ever! It also makes wonderful apple crisp and is terrific warmed and poured over vanilla ice cream. Making it brings back sweet memories. I remember as a child all of the family in the kitchen together canning. It has always been my favorite time of year...a time to talk and share the special moments of our lives.

4-1/2 c. sugar
3 T. cinnamon
1/4 t. nutmeg
10 c. water, divided
2 t. salt
1 c. cornstarch

3 T. lemon juice
6 lbs. cooking apples, cored, peeled and sliced
7 to 8 1-quart canning jars and lids, sterilized

In a large saucepan, mix sugar, cinnamon, nutmeg, 8 cups water and salt. Cook and stir over medium-high heat, about 10 minutes. Whisk together remaining water, cornstarch and lemon juice; add to sugar mixture. Cook over medium-low heat until syrup thickens, about 3 minutes. Fill hot sterilized jars with apple slices; ladle syrup into jars, leaving 1/2-inch headspace. Remove any bubbles with a knife. Wipe rims and secure lids and rings. Process in a boiling-water bath for 25 minutes. Set jars on a towel to cool. Check for seals. Makes 7 to 8 jars.

Make a pumpkin basket just like you would a watermelon basket! Use a mini saw to create the basket shape and handle, then remove the seeds and fill with florists' foam. Water the foam well and tuck in mums, sprigs of bittersweet and colorful fall leaves.

Carolyn's Blackberry Jelly

Carolyn Cochran
Dresden, OH

Every time I eat blackberry jelly, I remember the times I picked blackberries with my Grandparents Martin. It was back in the 1940s. They drove their bright green Plymouth Coupe to the blackberry patch that was on a hillside about one mile from my house. I would ride my bicycle and meet them there and we would pick berries all morning. I still love to pick berries, even though I am in my 70s.

6 qts. blackberries
1/4 to 1/2 c. water
3 c. sugar

1-3/4 oz. pkg. powdered pectin
5 1/2 pint canning jars and
   lids, sterilized

Cook blackberries in a large stockpot over medium-high heat for 10 to 20 minutes, or until soft. Strain berries through cheesecloth. Add enough water to strained juice to equal 4-1/2 cups; return to pot. Combine sugar and pectin and stir into juice. Stirring frequently, bring to a full boil and cook 5 to 10 minutes, or until jelly runs over the side of spoon in 2 sheets. Remove from heat; skim foam if needed and stir well. Spoon into hot sterilized jars, leaving 1/4-inch headspace. Wipe rims and secure lids and rings. Process in a boiling-water bath for 10 minutes. Set jars on a towel to cool. Check for seals. Makes 5 jars.

Spread spoonfuls of scrumptious jams, jellies and preserves on the flat sides of oatmeal cookies, then place the flat sides together. Wrap each yummy sandwich cookie in wax paper and tie with kitchen string. Nestle cookies inside a vintage cookie jar for a thoughtful gift sure to be remembered.

Vegetable Medley

*Margaret Scoresby
Mosinee, WI*

This makes a quick & easy side dish any time. Just mix & match your family's favorite vegetables and you can't go wrong. I'll also often sprinkle in dried herbs such as oregano, rosemary, basil, thyme and tarragon.

2 T. butter
1/4 c. onion, coarsely chopped
2 to 3 c. mixed vegetables,
  chopped
salt and pepper to taste

Optional: celery salt or garlic
  salt to taste
Optional: chicken broth
1-pint freezer-safe plastic
  container and lid, sterilized

Melt butter in a saucepan over medium heat; add onion and sauté 2 to 3 minutes. Add vegetables to onion mixture and heat through, stirring frequently. Add seasonings as desired; reduce heat to low and cook, covered, just until vegetables are tender. Add a small amount of broth if needed to prevent sticking. Spoon into a sterilized container, leaving about 1/4-inch headspace. Secure lid and freeze. Makes one container.

When peppers and onions are overflowing in the garden, here's a simple recipe you'll love. Slice and cook them in a little olive oil until tender, then pack in freezer-safe containers. When dinnertime calls for Italian sausages topped with peppers and onions, just pull a bag from the freezer and reheat on the stove or in the microwave.

Hot Dog Relish

Shannon Price
West Chester, PA

Or hamburger relish…you choose! Either way you can't go wrong with this tasty relish. We've even used it in homemade potato salad and macaroni salad.

6 cucumbers, finely chopped
1/4 c. salt
4 c. sweet onions, finely chopped
1 red pepper, finely chopped
2 c. white vinegar
2 c. sugar

3 T. all-purpose flour
1 t. dry mustard
1 t. mustard seed
1 t. celery seed
1 t. turmeric
4 1-pint canning jars and lids, sterilized

Place cucumbers in a large bowl; sprinkle with salt. Mix well, cover and refrigerate overnight. When ready to prepare, pour cucumber mixture and liquid into a large stockpot. Stir in remaining ingredients and cook over medium heat about 20 minutes. Spoon relish into hot sterilized jars, leaving 1/4-inch headspace. Wipe rims and secure lids and rings. Process in a boiling-water bath for 15 minutes. Set jars on a towel to cool. Check for seals. Makes 4 jars.

Halloween night is the perfect time to make hot dog "spiders" for a fun dinner surprise. Cut the ends of each hot dog into quarters, leaving about 2 inches in the middle uncut. Place a stick or skewer in the middle of each hot dog and roast over a fire or hot coals. The "legs" will curl as the hot dog cooks!

The Best Freezer Pickles

Barbara Feist Stienstra
Goshen, NY

This recipe is one of those tried & true ones that can be counted on when the cucumbers really begin to come in during high summer!

4 c. cucumbers, thinly sliced
Optional: 1 to 2 c. onion, thinly
   sliced
2 T. salt
2 T. water
1 c. sugar

1/2 c. cider vinegar
1 t. dill weed
4 1/2-pint freezer-safe
   plastic containers and lids,
   sterilized

Mix cucumbers, onion, salt and water. Let stand for 2 hours; drain. Return to bowl and add remaining ingredients. Let stand until sugar is dissolved and liquid covers vegetables, approximately 2 hours. Spoon into sterilized containers, leaving 1/2-inch headspace; secure lids and freeze. Thaw in refrigerator before using. Makes 4 containers.

Freeze whole bell peppers, it's easy! Just wash well, slice off the tops and remove the seeds. Wrap each pepper in aluminum foil, then place them in a freezer bag. Add your favorite stuffing to the peppers while they're still slightly frozen, or stuff them before freezing. What a time-saver!

Home Sweet HOMEMADE

Picture-Perfect Pumpkins

pumpkin	computer printer
pumpkin carving tools	hammer and large nail
digital photo	tacks or small nails
acetate sheet	battery-operated candle

Remove top and hollow out pumpkin, then set aside. Print a digital photo onto an acetate sheet (available at office supply stores) and measure photo. Cut an opening on the front of pumpkin that's slightly smaller than photo. Use a hammer and large nail to punch decorative holes into the pumpkin. Secure the photo to the pumpkin from the inside with tacks or small nails. Set a battery-operated candle inside the pumpkin and replace the top.

Knitted Coffee Cozy

size 10-1/2 (7mm) straight
   knitting needles
chunky wool yarn in 1 or
   2 colors

wool needle
hot-glue gun and glue stick
vintage earring, button or
   felted flower

For a one-color cozy, loosely cast on 22 stitches and knit 3 rows.
Purl one row and knit one row; repeat 2 more times for a total of
6 rows in stocking stitch. Knit 3 rows and bind off tightly, leaving
a long end. Use a wool needle to sew seam.

For a 2-color cozy, loosely cast on 22 stitches in main color. Knit
3 rows then change to secondary color. Purl one row and knit
one row; repeat 2 more times for a total of 6 rows in stocking stitch.
Change to main color and knit 3 rows; bind off tightly, leaving a
long end. Use a wool needle to sew seam.

Use a hot-glue gun to attach a vintage earring or stitch on a button
or a felted flower.

Harvest Table Runner

1 to 2 yds. burlap
fabric scraps
scissors

straight pins
double-sided fusible webbing
iron and ironing board

Place burlap on table, cutting so it covers the middle third of the table. If desired, fray the edges by gently pulling away 1/2 inch of burlap, one strand at a time. Pin fabric scraps to fusible webbing and cut into pumpkin or leaf shapes, or letters to create a monogram. Arrange shapes on the burlap, fusible webbing-side down. Carefully remove the pins, keeping the fabric and webbing together. Following the fusible webbing manufacturer's instructions, use a warm iron to adhere the webbing to the pieces of burlap.

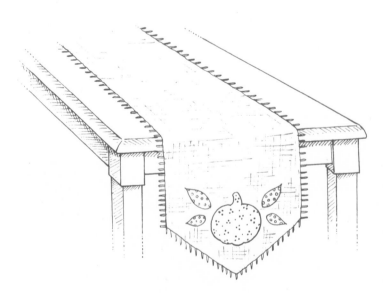

Silly Scarecrone

hollow foam pumpkin	one wood screw
pumpkin carving tools	old full slip, dress, apron
4-foot 1"x2" wooden stake	and hat
6-foot 2"x4" wooden stake	hay
saw	staple gun
drill	mallet

Carve a face out of the foam pumpkin using pumpkin carving tools; set aside. So that dress will fit, trim the vertical piece a few inches shorter than span of the sleeves. Create a cross, laying the shorter stake horizontally across longer one, and 6 inches from the top. Drill a hole through the center of cross; insert wood screw to secure stakes together. Place slip and dress over vertical stake, slide horizontal stake through sleeves. Stuff slip and sleeves with hay, leaving about 6 inches of space at bottom of the slip. Gather slip tightly around stake; staple to secure. Use the mallet to secure the stake in the ground. Fill foam pumpkin head with hay and place on scarecrone. Tie on apron and add a hat.

Boo-tiful Candy Wrapper Pail

paintbrush
découpage medium

tin bucket
candy wrappers

Use a paintbrush to apply découpage medium to outside of the bucket. While still wet, arrange candy wrappers on surface of bucket. Reapply découpage medium to the surface and let dry.

Pumpkin Votives

mini pumpkins
candle wicks with clips

shredded candle wax
saucepan

Hollow out mini pumpkins and make a small cut in the bottom of each pumpkin. Push clip end of the wick into skin of the pumpkin so wick stands up straight. In a medium saucepan, melt wax over low heat until it's clear. Slowly pour wax
into each pumpkin, keeping the wick upright.
When wax has completely cooled, trim the wicks.

Home Sweet Homemade

Blooming Mum Pin

fabric scraps
liquid starch
button

scissors
needle and thread
jewelry pin or safety pin

Following manufacturer's instructions, heavily starch fabric scraps
with liquid starch. Using the pattern below as a guide, copy the
pattern in 4 different sizes onto a sheet of paper. Cut out at least
2 pieces of fabric in each size. Stack and arrange fabric into a flower
shape, fanning out the different sizes. Place a button in the center
of the top fabric and sew through the layers. Stitch a jewelry pin or
safety pin on the back.

Haunted House

pint-size paper milk carton
cardboard square
vanilla frosting
graham crackers
candy corn

black licorice
mini chocolate bars
candy pumpkins
ghost-shaped marshmallows

Clean out the milk carton with soapy water, rinse and let dry. Attach the milk carton to the cardboard square with a dollop of frosting; hold in place for 30 seconds. Use frosting to attach graham crackers to carton, breaking the crackers as needed to fit. To form the roof, turn 2 graham cracker rectangles on their sides and lean toward each other; secure to the carton with frosting. Cut a cracker square diagonally and attach each piece to the front and back of the roof. Use frosting to attach the remaining candy. Use candy corn as shingles and mini chocolate bars as doors and windows. Use black licorice to fill in the seams of the house and attach pumpkins and ghost-shaped marshmallows.

Apple Wreath

8-inch length heavy-gauge
   wire
Scented Apples

pliers
thin floral wire
ribbon bow

Form the wire into a heart shape. Fold the Scented Apples into halves, then into quarters and thread onto the wire. Use pliers to bend the wire ends into hooks and connect them. Use floral wire to attach a ribbon and create a loop for hanging.

Scented Apples:

8 to 10 firm apples like
   Braeburn or Granny Smith
1-1/2 c. lemon juice
2 t. salt

2 T. cinnamon
2 t. allspice
1 t. ground cloves

Peel and slice apples horizontally into 1/4-inch thick pieces; core slices as needed. In a medium bowl, combine lemon juice and salt. Soak apples in lemon juice mixture for 6 minutes, turning once. Drain apples and pat dry. Combine spices. Dust apples with spice mixture; gently remove excess with a pastry brush. Arrange slices in a single layer on a broiler pan and dry in a 200-degree oven for 6 hours, or until evenly dried. Slices will be pliable.

Porch Pumpkin Tower

black permanent marker
7 pumpkins in graduated sizes,
   stems removed
6-quart galvanized bucket
5- to 6-foot wooden stake

sand
knife
assorted gourds and mini
   pumpkins

Use a permanent marker to write one letter per pumpkin, to spell out
"WELCOME." Place the stake upright in a bucket; fill the bucket
with sand to secure the stake in place. Use a knife to cut small entry
holes in the bottoms of the pumpkins. Stack the pumpkins on the
stake, starting with the largest. Arrange
gourds and mini pumpkins at the base
of the stake. Place near your front door
to greet guests and goblins!

Indian Corn Pin

4-1/2 inch yellow chenille stem
2-1/3 inch yellow chenille stem
18 plastic tri-beads in fall
   colors
craft glue

2-1/2 yds. raffia
craft wire
5 inches 1/4-inch wide ribbon
jewelry pin

Fold longer chenille stem in half; wrap one end of shorter stem around the fold to make 3 prongs. Thread beads onto prongs in random order. Place a drop of craft glue in the hole of the last bead on each prong; let dry. Cut 20 pieces of raffia 4-1/2 inches long. Fold 10 raffia pieces between the first and second prongs; repeat for between the second and third prongs. Pull the raffia together and secure with craft wire to hold it tightly together; twist ends and clip. Hide the wire by adding a ribbon tied in a bow. Attach the jewelry pin with glue; let dry.

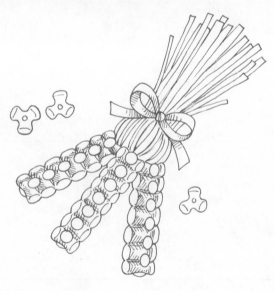

Sparkly Pumpkins

2 paintbrushes
craft glue
3 pumpkins
orange, red and clear craft
   glitter

brown acrylic paint
cake pedestals

Use a paintbrush to evenly apply glue
over the surface of one pumpkin.
Choose one glitter and sprinkle glitter
over the glue, covering it completely.
Repeat, using a different color of glitter for
remaining pumpkins. Let dry for one hour;
shake off excess glitter. Paint the stems
with the brown acrylic paint and let dry.
Arrange the pumpkins on cake pedestals
for a festive centerpiece.

Framed Fall Greeting

colored paper
picture frame
calligraphy pen, crayons,
   markers

pressed leaves
double-sided tape

Trim colored paper to fit inside the
frame. Use a calligraphy pen to
write "Welcome" or "Greetings"
along the top third of the paper. You
can also have the kids use crayons
or markers to write the greeting.
Using double-sided tape, attach
pressed leaves to the paper and
slip the paper into the frame.

Hostess Gift Coasters & Potholder

4 3-1/2 inch dia. circles Felted
   Wool pieces
needle and embroidery thread
2 8-1/2 inch squares Felted
   Wool pieces

straight pins
size 20 chenille needle
worsted-weight wool knitting
   yarn

For coasters, use a needle and thread to sew a straight-stitch border along each of the circle-shaped pieces, 1/4 inch from the edge. For potholder, pin the square pieces, wrong sides together. Stitch squares together using a chenille needle and wool yarn to sew a blanket stitch to attach the 2 pieces.

Felted Wool:

washing machine
100% wool fabric
zippered laundry bag

liquid laundry detergent
clothes dryer

Set up washing machine for heavy-duty cycle with hot-water wash. Place wool fabric in a zippered laundry bag. Add detergent (1/3 capful for small load; 1/2 capful for medium; 3/4 capful for large). Wash fabric with the full machine cycle. Machine dry on high setting of clothes dryer. Cut felted wool to desired size.

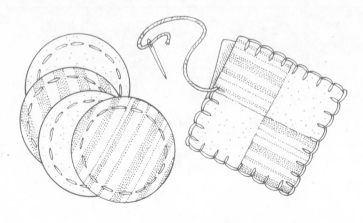

Elegant Leaf Tray Liners

wax paper
rectangular tray
various dried leaves

iron and ironing board
tea towel

Cut 2 sheets of wax paper to fit the bottom of the tray. Arrange leaves on one sheet of paper and cover with the other sheet. Lay on an ironing board and cover with a tea towel. With the iron on the low-heat setting, carefully iron the wax paper until the 2 sheets stick together. Line a serving tray with the finished liner.

Halloween Party Tub

16-gallon galvanized metal
  wash tub
orange spray paint for metal
  surfaces
tracing paper
cardstock or other thick paper

craft knife
tape
black acrylic paint
paintbrush
old toothbrush
spray polyurethane

Spray outside of tub with orange paint; let dry. To create a stencil,
draw pumpkin eyes, nose and mouth onto tracing paper and cut
out. Transfer cutouts to cardstock and cut each carefully with
a craft knife. Tape stencil to tub and use black paint to stencil on
the face; let dry. Dip an old toothbrush into black paint thinned
with a little water. Position the toothbrush over the tub; drag your
thumbnail or palette knife across the bristles to spatter the surface.
Let dry. To protect paint, coat the outside of the tub with
polyurethane. Fill with ice and beverages or with water and
apples for apple bobbing.

Terra-Cotta Bread Pots

5 new 6-inch terra-cotta
   flower pots
parchment paper
3-lb. pkg. frozen bread dough
   (5 count), thawed

1 egg white
1 T. water
Garnish: all-purpose flour,
   caraway seed, poppy seed,
   oats

Wash pots in hot soapy water, thoroughly rinse and let dry
completely. Trace the bottom of the pots onto parchment paper and
cut the circles out. Place a circle in the bottom of each pot. Spray
the inside of the pots with non-stick vegetable spray. Place one
piece of dough into each pot and spray tops of dough with non-stick
vegetable spray. Place pots, uncovered, on bottom rack of a cold
oven. Place a small pan of boiling water in the oven. Close oven
door and let bread rise until double in bulk, about 20 minutes.
Remove pots and water from oven. Combine egg white with water
and brush evenly over the loaves. Sprinkle loaves with desired
garnish. Bake pots on bottom oven rack at 375 degrees for
30 minutes, until golden. Cool on wire racks.

Tin-Can Luminaries

tracing paper
clean, empty tin cans of
   various sizes
permanent marker
hammer and large nail

ruler
Optional: 16" craft wire
   spray paint for metal surfaces
    in color of your choice
tealight candles

Trace fall patterns such as bats, leaves or pumpkin faces onto tracing paper that will fit tin cans. Cut out patterns and arrange on the cans; outline with a permanent marker. Fill each can with water and place in the freezer until water is completely frozen. Remove from freezer and punch dotted lines along designs using a hammer and nail. If hanging lanterns are desired, punch 2 holes in the rim of the can on opposite sides. Let ice melt and cans dry completely. For the optional handle, insert wire into the holes along the rim; twist ends to secure. Spray paint the outside of the cans and let dry. Place a candle in each can.

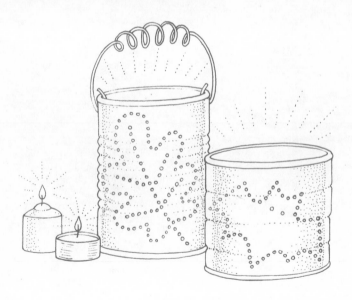

INDEX

INDEX

INDEX

Send us your favorite recipe!

and the memory that makes it special for you!* If we select your recipe for a brand-new **Gooseberry Patch** cookbook, your name will appear right along with it...and you'll receive a FREE copy of the book.

Share your recipe on our website at
www.gooseberrypatch.com

Or mail to:

Gooseberry Patch · Attn: Cookbook Dept.
P.O. Box 190 · Delaware, OH 43015

*Don't forget to include your name, address, phone number and email address so we'll know how to reach you for your FREE book!

Since 1992, we've been publishing country cookbooks for every kitchen and for every meal of the day! Each has hundreds of budget-friendly recipes, using ingredients you already have on hand. Their lay-flat binding makes them easy to use and each is filled with hand-drawn artwork and plenty of personality.

Have a taste for more?

Call us toll-free at
1·800·854·6673

Find us here too!

Join our **Circle of Friends** and discover free recipes & crafts, plus giveaways & more! Visit our website or blog to join and be sure to follow us on Facebook & Twitter too.

www.gooseberrypatch.com

Join Our Circle of Friends

VIDEOS

Read Our Blog

f Find us on Facebook

Follow us on twitter

U.S. to Canadian recipe equivalents

Volume Measurements

1/4 teaspoon	1 mL
1/2 teaspoon	2 mL
1 teaspoon	5 mL
1 tablespoon = 3 teaspoons	15 mL
2 tablespoons = 1 fluid ounce	30 mL
1/4 cup	60 mL
1/3 cup	75 mL
1/2 cup = 4 fluid ounces	125 mL
1 cup = 8 fluid ounces	250 mL
2 cups = 1 pint =16 fluid ounces	500 mL
4 cups = 1 quart	1 L

Weights

1 ounce	30 g
4 ounces	120 g
8 ounces	225 g
16 ounces = 1 pound	450 g

Oven Temperatures

300° F	150° C
325° F	160° C
350° F	180° C
375° F	190° C
400° F	200° C
450° F	230° C

Baking Pan Sizes

Square

8x8x2 inches	2 L = 20x20x5 cm
9x9x2 inches	2.5 L = 23x23x5 cm

Rectangular

13x9x2 inches	3.5 L = 33x23x5 cm

Loaf

9x5x3 inches	2 L = 23x13x7 cm

Round

8x1-1/2 inches	1.2 L = 20x4 cm
9x1-1/2 inches	1.5 L = 23x4 cm